THE KNOWLEDGE OF REALITY

THE KNOWLEDGE OF REALITY

By

WINCENTY LUTOSŁAWSKI

CAMBRIDGE
AT THE UNIVERSITY PRESS
1930

CAMBRIDGE
UNIVERSITY PRESS

University Printing House, Cambridge CB2 8BS, United Kingdom

Cambridge University Press is part of the University of Cambridge.

It furthers the University's mission by disseminating knowledge in the pursuit of education, learning and research at the highest international levels of excellence.

www.cambridge.org
Information on this title: www.cambridge.org/9781107455689

© Cambridge University Press 1930

First published 1930
First paperback edition 2014

A catalogue record for this publication is available from the British Library

ISBN 978-1-107-45568-9 Paperback

TO EVA AND MARJORIE,
FRIENDS OF MANY LIVES,
THIS WORK SHOULD APPEAR
AS THEIR OWN, BEING BORN
OF OUR MEMORABLE TALKS
IN CARBIS BAY, AUGUST 1928

PREFACE

This is the outline of a course of metaphysics, given first at the University of Kazan (1890–93), then at Cracow (1899–1907), at Geneva (1912–16), at the Sorbonne in Paris (1919), at the University of Wilno (1919–29), at the University of Posen (1921), at the Universities of Warsaw and Lwów (1923) and on many other occasions elsewhere. The theory of matter was first published in Polish in June 1921 in the *Nowy Przegląd Literatury i Sztuki* (Warszawa, Bibljoteka Polska), and then in English in July 1929 in the quarterly, *The Monist*, Chicago. The full course contained in addition a theory of personality, of which the first chapter appeared in Jan. 1922 in vol. XXXI (N. 121) of *Mind*. The full Theory of Personality will form a sequel to this and the two preceding works of the author, *The World of Souls* (1924) and *Pre-existence and Reincarnation* (1928).

These four volumes and a work already written on the *Discovery of God* form one whole, the final outcome of a life devoted to the understanding of Reality. It seems that the need of such an understanding is steadily growing, though the last great synthetic effort of Charles Renouvier, who, having passed his 86th birthday, gave in four volumes 1899–1903 the results of his thought, remains little known outside a small circle of readers in France.

In England the thinker whose works in many respects show the closest relation to my own thought is Dr F. A. M. Spencer, to whom I am greatly indebted for the care expended on the manuscript and proofs of my two latest works. His exceptionally valuable suggestions have greatly improved my text and I should like all my readers to become acquainted with his works, which may be considered as a spontaneous English confirmation of Polish thought.

In his *Meaning of Christianity* (T. Fisher Unwin, 1912, 2nd ed. revised, 1914) he shows that each soul must pass through many incarnations, so as to develop, in union with God, that spiritual life which will eventually enable it to overcome death. In *Human Ideals* (T. Fisher Unwin, 1917) he indicates how all human progress should be directed to the birth and development of this spiritual life. He emphasizes the persistent solidarity of the individual ego with human society, both national and international, so that only through the perfecting of humanity as the Kingdom of God can each human being become perfect as a child of God.[1]

---

[1] The other works of Dr Spencer are: (1) *The Ethics of the Gospel*, in which he makes a brief survey of the ethical teaching of Jesus and indicates its bearings upon modern life, handling the themes with a wise and scholarly frankness which makes it most interesting reading; (2) *Civilization Remade by Christ*, in which he shows that this teaching contains principles for the solution of many of the main problems of civilization. Here he combines a wide treatment of great themes with concreteness of handling and definite reference to the teaching of Jesus; (3) *The*

That Poland may have a message for the English-speaking world is after all not more surprising than the acknowledged truth that Palestine had a message for the Roman Empire, which needed three centuries to be accepted. I hope the Polish message will reach its goal more easily, as it is merely an expansion of the old Gospel truth.

My preceding books have created a stream of personal correspondence from readers, which I value very much. I appeal to the wider circle of readers of this book to make themselves similarly known, so that, since contemporary life on the whole is tending in the opposite direction, I may gauge the effect produced by this voice in the wilderness.

W. LUTOSŁAWSKI

JAGIELLOŃSKA 7, m. 2

WILNO, POLAND.

April 2, 1930.

Theory of Christ's Ethics, in which he gives a deeper and more detailed treatment of the Gospel ethics. He argues that Jesus had in view a thorough reconstruction of society, including the formation of an international brotherhood for securing peace. He demonstrates the psychological truth of the attitude of Jesus to the great instincts of human nature and of his diagnosis of moral maladies. He relates the ethics of Jesus to His offer of redemption and eternal life. Finally, he indicates how the philosophical conception of absolute value and the *summum bonum* is elucidated by the great ideal of Jesus, which He called "the Kingdom of God". In all these points Dr Spencer wonderfully confirms the teaching of the Polish philosopher Cieszkowski, whom he certainly did not know when writing the above three volumes, published by Messrs Allen and Unwin since 1925.

CONTENTS

CONTENTS

CONTENTS

xiv

CONTENTS

xvi

CONTENTS

Chapter XVII: REGENERATED MANKIND 175-181

Very small states are likely to disappear—Greater states will be formed, **175**. Public instruction is not a business of the State—number of officials reduced, **176**. Big cities superfluous—Decentralisation of industry—Useful production—the British Museum more durable than most houses around it, **177**. Private initiative and creative genius will prevail—Disappearance of physicians, lawyers and clergymen, **178**. Transformation of domestic service—No working men as a class—Need of leisure, **179**. Ladies and gentlemen of leisure will be inspired workers—Immortal bodies—Birth, death and procreation no longer needed—Life without violence, anger, fear, hate, envy, calumny, strife, **180**. Life of sanctity and genius, **181**.

Chapter XVIII: THE IMMEDIATE OUTLOOK   182-190

Sir Francis Younghusband presupposes a group of gifted individuals in one place, **182**. Messianic school educating such workers—Method of work in a Forge, **183**. Messianic press—History rewritten, **184**. Increase of biographical literature—Continuous action of Providence—International organisation increases—Mankind grows towards unity, **185**. *The Times Literary Supplement*—Creation of a home for the new spirit, **186**. A new kind of love—A school and a monastery with a laboratory in the mountains—Practical plan of activity, **187**. Ultimate test of Messianism—A way of escape from the present misery—Workshop for the Great Transformation—The wealthy are not likely to furnish the means, **188**. A great opportunity for Mr Ford—Alice in Wonderland may work miracles—Each of us can improve himself and the condition of life for his neighbour, **189**. The number of such men is rapidly increasing—the application of metaphysics to social and political activity necessary, **190**.

CHAPTER I

Classification of Philosophers

It is surprising that even among those who devote their lives to philosophy very few seek a synthetic view of the whole of existence, and among the few who desire this, still fewer attempt to formulate their own and the universal experience into a clear outline of True Being.

We have in neither English, French, Italian, nor Spanish, a simple term for what a German calls *Weltanschauung*, a Pole *Światopogląd*, a Russian *Mirosoziercanije*. Such a term is increasingly needed as the interest in metaphysical speculation grows, and hungry souls are too often fed with the many spurious products of arrogant ignorance. The modesty of genuine thinkers, aware of the difficulties of such an undertaking, prevents them from offering the general reader a definite answer to such burning questions as: 'What really exists?'

For centuries the answer given by religions was sufficient for the majority of mankind. But every religion is based upon a revelation vouchsafed to a few, and exacting blind faith from the many. Now these blind masses want to think for themselves, and they are mostly misled by false prophets.

Expert philosophers are usually absorbed in details of historical or methodological research, or they limit their account of Being to such abstractions as have scant interest for the seeker after concrete realities. Such a failure was, for instance, a book published in 1876 by the famous Italian philosopher Terenzio Mamiani, under the very promising title *Compendio e sintesi della propria filosofia*. We read nearly three hundred pages without learning anything about individual beings and their relations. The author is lost in his contemplation of the Absolute.

The example of Renouvier who, when over eighty years of age, published four large volumes in order to give the ultimate conclusions of his life experience is quite unique in the twentieth century. And those who have on a smaller scale given their view of the whole of life have not attempted to survey exhaustively the real alternatives in philosophy.

Almost every thinker writes as if his own solution of the riddle of existence were the only one deserving any attention, and as if there were no problem of a classification of possible conceptions. We still find in every century materialists and idealists who mutually despise one another, and pantheists who consider both materialism and idealism as affording too narrow a conception of Being. Names are invented in every generation for new philosophies called either after their author or according to his outstanding dogma.

Some few thinkers have attempted to deal with this problem of classification, among them Renouvier in his *Esquisse d'une classification systématique des doctrines philosophiques* (2 vols. Paris, 1885–1886) and Ernest Naville in his *Philosophies affirmatives* (Paris, 1909). The present author has a like aim, and desires to show how the age-long quest for truth has gradually exhausted various possibilities, and has led to a final synthesis, revealing the ultimate nature of material, intellectual and spiritual existence.

If the reader follows the indications resulting from past adventures in the realm of ends,[1] he will be able to make his own choice of a point of view, and to stop at any convenient resting-place before reaching what the author considers as his own goal.

As we shall have to deal with metaphysical alternatives usually called 'conceptions of existence', let us introduce a term to define such an aspect of Being. There is a rare Greek word, unknown to Liddell and Scott (at least in an edition of 1873 which I have consulted), but used by the philosopher Porphyry in his work *de Abstinentia* (mentioned in the Greek-French dictionary of M. A. Bailly, Paris, Hachette, 1899). This word is *theasis*, meaning 'the act of vision', or 'contemplation'. It is akin to 'theory' and might well express 'view of existence', 'synthetical conception of the whole'. Let us introduce 'theasy' as the only neologism to which the author pleads

[1] See James Ward, *The Realm of Ends*.

3   1-2

guilty, whereas German philosophers create new terms according to Mephisto's saying: 'wo der Begriff fehlt, da stellt das Wort sich ein'.

Now we may ask how many possible theasies have ever existed, and how we can classify them. Every theasy depends on two factors: first, the subject who looks at the world; and secondly, the object or world which he contemplates.

This object is by no means always the same for all thinkers. There is an enormous variety of personal experience and nobody knows more than a very small part of the whole. But in that particular part everybody seeks to discover what it has in common with the whole, and what is most likely to be accessible to all men.

Therefore the real alternatives depend much more on the quality of the subject than on the various aspects of the object. There is a limited number of fundamental human types corresponding to the chief metaphysical alternatives in our understanding of reality.

These types of men are not equal to one another, but form an ascending hierarchy like organic species in the process of biological evolution. The best way to distinguish between them is to consider the prevailing contents of their consciousness. If man wishes to judge reality, he cannot help using his own mind as a test of the whole universe.

The chief contents of every mind are sensations,

4

thoughts, emotions and volitions. But the proportions of these psychemas vary. The vast majority of men anywhere are those in whom sensations prevail over everything else.

The object of sensations is matter, and it is natural for the man of sensations to imagine all existence as material. Such a man we call a *materialist* and his theasy *materialism*.

Others care infinitely more for the activity of thought—consisting in notions, judgments, inferences —than for sensations. They are prone to imagine that everything is thought, and that nothing can exist except ideas. We call such thinkers *idealists*.

The man of ideas belongs to an altogether different type from the man of sensations. Idealists and materialists have argued for centuries without ever convincing one another. Materialism and idealism are the two most obvious solutions of the riddle of existence, and the immense majority of living men are either materialists or idealists.

But there is a third type of man, who creates a different theasy. He is more interested in his emotions than in either sensations or thoughts. For certain reasons which will be given below we shall call him a *pantheist*. If will prevails over emotions, thoughts and sensations, then a fourth type of theasy appears, called *spiritualism*.

These four theasies—materialism, idealism, pantheism, and spiritualism—are those best known in the history of philosophy, and Ernest Naville considers them the only possible alternatives. Whether he is right we shall be able to judge if we compare this psychological classification of fundamental types with the evidence of history.

This will enable us also to see how each theasy forms one stage in the general quest for truth, so that the human spirit ascends from stage to stage, conscious of widening horizons, to a final synthesis which will provide the ultimate answer to our doubts. No single point of view can give us a guarantee of objectivity. We need to compare them all, and to understand how they are related to each other, before we can decide what is the outcome of all philosophical research into the mystery of True Being.

Then perhaps it will appear that Naville's classification, though true, is not complete, and that there are some stages beyond spiritualism, pantheism, idealism, and materialism. Still, this preliminary classification, based on the predominance of one or other of the chief factors of consciousness, enables us to group philosophers under four main headings, and embraces very nearly the whole history of human thought, as a brief historical survey will easily show.

CHAPTER II

Materialism

The most common types of men are those in whom sensations prevail over everything else. The object of sensations is matter, and it is natural for the man of sensations to imagine that all existence is material. Such a man we call a *materialist*, and his view of existence is called *materialism*.

Materialism is the oldest theory of Being, known for more than twenty-four centuries in Europe, and very likely for a still longer time in the East. Its birth and development in Greece deserve our close attention. It is in vain that some historians of philosophy have invented such names as *hylozoism* in order to disguise the origin of European materialism. It remains a fact that, according to our definition, the oldest known European philosopher, Thales (about 624–546 B.C.), was a materialist, as he thought that everything had its origin in water and that water was the hidden reality of everything. We can easily explain his theasy by his most familiar perceptions. He lived in the seaport Miletus, and his attention was naturally attracted to the sea. Pondering on its immensity with awe, a man for whom sensations were the chief source of knowledge was naturally led to the generalisation that water was the chief reality, the hidden essence of all reality.

His follower Anaximander (about 610–546 B.C.) went one step further by postulating an undefined material principle of the universe, which he named *apeiron*, the Unknown or Infinite. He accepted from Thales the notion of a primitive unity of all matter, out of which everything originated through eternal movement. The third Milesian thinker, Anaximenes (about 585–525 B.C.), agreed with Thales and Anaximander in the conception of a first material principle, which, however, he concretely identified as air, subject to both condensation and rarefaction, and producing fire, water and earth.

For Heraclitus (about 536–470 B.C.) the first and last material principle was fire, in continual movement. Empedocles (about 483–413 B.C.) introduced into materialism a pluralistic conception of several first principles, whereby he went a step further than the Ionians, though his four elements—earth, water, air and fire—were the same as theirs. His definition of the energy which moves matter as *love* and *hate* is only apparently psychological, since for him love is nothing else than a force that unites material things, and hate is the force of dissociation.

Anaxagoras (about 499–428 B.C.) extends materialistic pluralism beyond Empedocles to an indefinite number of qualitatively different elements called *homœomeries* (having parts similar to each other), but he calls the moving energy *reason*, whereby he already transcends pure materialism.

In opposition to the qualitative pluralism of Anaxagoras appears the quantitative pluralism, or atomism, of Democritus (about 460–370 B.C.). To him every qualitative difference is produced by the movements of unchangeable atoms and he has no name for the moving energy, as he considers movement eternal, without beginning or end. Numberless worlds follow each other, and the soul of each man consists of fire-atoms, distributed throughout the body.

This form of materialism, however crude, remained for many centuries almost unchanged. When Thales said that everything was water, he was a more consistent materialist than Democritus when he sought to explain everything by invisible and impalpable atoms, moving in infinite space through the eternity of time. We do not really perceive the atoms, nor infinite space, nor infinite time. Thus atomists also transcend pure materialism by introducing abstract notions into their theasy.

The hold of materialism over the common mind is shown by the stupendous fact that after the short interval of idealism taught by Plato and Aristotle, the two foremost ethical schools of Epicureans and Stoics, who divided between them the seekers after truth in the Greco-Roman world until the advent of Christianity and for several succeeding centuries, remained materialistic in their conception of the universe, like their predecessors the Cynics and the Cyrenaics.

Antisthenes (about 436–366 B.C.), the founder of the Cynic school, believed that souls have the same shape as bodies, which implies that they are material. Zeno (336–264 B.C.), who transformed cynicism into stoicism, and ended his life by suicide, remained a materialist, for he looked upon the soul and even God as material. Aristippus (435–356 B.C.), the founder of the Cyrenaic school of hedonists, explained pleasure and pain by the movement of matter, like his successors in the Cyrenaic school, Theodorus the Atheist and Hegesias Peisithanatos, who led many of their followers to suicide.

Epicurus (341–271 B.C.) introduced into atomism a curious novelty, namely an arbitrary and accidental change in the direction of the atomic movements, in order to justify the freedom of will. But he taught, like his predecessors, that the soul consists of atoms of fire and air, distributed throughout the whole body.

Thus materialism prevailed in the most popular Socratic schools for centuries. The Roman Lucretius (96–55 B.C.), in his famous epic *De Rerum natura*, immortalised the doctrine of Epicurus and has been read by materialists for nearly twenty centuries.

The rise of Christianity introduced into the consciousness of the masses an anti-materialistic tendency.

But in the writings of even so passionate a Christian as Tertullian (A.D. 160-240) it is not difficult to find thoroughly materialistic passages. Also Augustine (354-430) confessed (*Confessions*, lib. VII) that it had been to him for a long time almost impossible to understand immaterial existence. But no eminent materialist appeared after Lucretius until Thomas Hobbes (1588-1679) published his *Elementa philosophiæ* (1652), to a certain extent anticipated by the inductive and experimental philosophy of Francis Bacon (1561-1626). It is a very remarkable fact in the history of human thought that materialism, being the natural point of view of the majority of mankind up to the present time, could have been silenced for more than sixteen centuries by the spread of Christianity.

During this period there were many materialists of lower rank, such as Nicolas d'Autrecourt, who in 1347 had to withdraw his assertion that nothing exists except the movement of atoms; or Laurentius Valla (1407-1457), whose work *De voluptate* (1431) is a defence of Epicureanism; but they had no influence and scarcely dared openly to proclaim their convictions.

It was only when the Christian faith was weakened by dissensions among Christians that materialism reappeared with renewed force, taking sometimes other names because of the general contempt into which it had been brought by Christian philosophy.

Thus it happened that in France a foremost materialist, contemporary of Hobbes, Pierre Gassendi (1592–1655), could remain a Catholic priest; he gave to his chief work, *Syntagma philosophiæ Epicuri* (published in Holland in 1659, after the author's death, and many times afterwards), the character of a historic investigation. Neither Hobbes nor Gassendi altered in any essential way the materialism of Epicurus, but Hobbes had the merit of drawing with consistency the political conclusions implied by materialism, and of recognising the despotic power of the State as a result of the materialistic view of nature.

The empiricism of John Locke (1632–1704) reaches opposite conclusions in political theory, but gives to the senses such pre-eminence that in our classification we must consider Locke as belonging to the materialist type, though he is not so thoroughly consistent as Hobbes.

The theism of John Toland (1670–1722) is also a slightly disguised materialism. The identification of psychology with physiology attempted by David Hartley (1705–1757) and Joseph Priestley (1733–1804) betrays the same tendency. In France, Pierre Bayle (1647–1706) inaugurated a new wave of materialism, of which the most famous exponents were: de la Mettrie (1709–1751), Baron Holbach (1723–1789) and Cabanis (1757–1808), among many others.

The sensualism of Condillac (1715–1780), though

he admits an immaterial soul, leads his readers inevitably to materialism, as does also the positivism of Auguste Comte (1798–1857).

They all agree with Epicurus on one essential point, in so far as they believe sensations to be the source of all knowledge, and in that respect we must class them as materialists.

In France materialism was overcome in the nineteenth century by a deeper philosophy, while in Germany a strong revival of materialism was produced by such writers as Carl Vogt (1817–1895), Jacob Moleschott (1822–1893), Ludwig Büchner (1824–1899), Heinrich Czolbe (1819–1873) and Ernst Haeckel (1834–1919). Haeckel has invented a new name for the same eternal theasy of Epicurus and Democritus—he calls his materialism *monism*. But this term has a wider meaning and includes theasies contrary to materialism.

On the whole, in the twentieth century, materialism as a professed doctrine is on the decline, but individual materialists remain numerous, especially among those whose calling necessitates the concentration of attention on material appearances; such are physicians, naturalists, engineers, and men of business. All such practical men, paying more attention to matter than to thought, are liable to generalise and to imagine that the only possible reality is matter. There is a materialism in ethics called utilitarianism and even a materialism in religious worship, when ritual is placed above prayer as the essential religious activity.

We cannot expect all materialists to be consistent and to deny emphatically the freedom of the will or the existence of God. But their God is a material conception, and their will is an activity of the nerves. They look upon the material world as the only reality, sensations as the source of knowledge, satisfaction of the senses as the condition of happiness.

Such men are proud of their common-sense and they claim to know for certain what is real: i.e. only what strikes the senses and produces sensations, followed by perceptions. They avoid the discredited term of materialism, and use many and various names to designate their theasy—such as sensualism, positivism, the philosophy of common-sense, criticism, empiricism, scientific method, etc.

In recent times materialism has sometimes been disguised in the teachings of certain schools of spurious mysticism—occultism, spiritism, and the like. Here lies distinct danger of confusion of mind, through the conceiving of spiritual truths in the guise of material symbolism, e.g. subconscious regions, astral planes, mental bodies, and so on.

Every believer in majorities applies materialist views to political life, and the classic national economy of Adam Smith, as well as modern socialism, betray equally the materialist attitude.

Materialism permeates our public life, literature

and art, in various unexpected ways, and with such inconsistencies that many materialists of a subtler kind are not aware of their fundamental agreement with the grosser, discredited materialism of the followers of traditional Epicureanism.

But within the last twenty-two centuries nobody has added anything to the Epicurean image of small bodies in movement as the materialistic explanation of reality, and this old theasy has won an increased authority by its use in modern sciences, which have become merely the investigation of the movements of small and large bodies. What these material bodies are, scientific research does not reveal, being concerned throughout with the ultimate fact that bodies exist and move in space and time, as a short survey of the scientific theory of matter will show us.

CHAPTER III

The Scientific Theory of Matter

The age-long existence of materialism as a philosophical theasy has deeply influenced scientific research, which had for its object the material world or that kind of presumed reality which strikes our senses.

Generally science has been regarded as the only means of understanding the nature of matter. Still the particular sciences are not all on a level, but form an ascending scale of efforts towards a fuller knowledge of different aspects of the material world.

The oldest of the natural sciences is astronomy. Observation of the stars shows us large bodies moving in unlimited space. This primitive image of shining points in presumed movement is an object of sight, and we conceive of all the matter in the visible universe as of a system of shining points.

This is the basis of the whole atomic conception, which claims to explain what is happening in the universe by the movement of infinitely small bodies in space. Each star being to human sight a mere small point almost without dimensions, the primitive astronomer had no inducement to probe deeper and to investigate the inner constitution of each star. The star is for him the ultimate unit of matter, and as far as sight goes, it is the smallest body in space. He cannot see the movement of such a body; he notices only from time to time a change in its position, and infers that a movement has taken place, similar in kind to the movements of shining meteors traversing our atmosphere. The sight of these shooting stars led to the more general conception of the uniform movements of all stars through practically infinite space. This is the astronomical conception of matter, resulting from the observations of the oldest natural science.

If a body is sufficiently small, the question of the inner structure or quality of that body appears to be superfluous, and the only quality left is movement. As time went on it was discovered that stars are not small bodies, but are mostly larger than the earth; this did not, however, change anything in the primitive scheme.

'A body in movement' seemed to be a sufficient answer to the question—What is matter? Yet a body must consist of some quantity of matter, so that each body, however small, contains the whole problem of matter, and this body's movement is no explanation of what matter is. However, atomism takes it for granted that movement explains everything, and that matter is simply minute bodies in movement.

Between the astronomic conception of matter and that of the physicist there is no other difference than that of dimensions. The astronomer looks at the whole universe accessible to our view; the physicist divides every minutest quantity of visible matter into invisible particles. The stars are visible, the molecules are invisible; the astronomer perceives matter only by sight, while the physicist is concerned with sensations different from those of sight, namely sounds, and electric and magnetic phenomena, producing impressions on the human nerves.

Thus it might be expected that the matter of the physicist would be more differentiated and complicated than that of the astronomer. Physical science seems to be at a more advanced stage in the scientific investigation of matter than astronomy, and farther from immediate sensation.

But strangely enough the physicist accepts the visual astronomical conception of matter integrally, and makes no use whatever of his other sensations. He transforms sounds into waves of molecules in movement, and conceives of electricity and magnetism in the same way.

His conception of matter as 'bodies in movement' is essentially the same as that of astronomy, and the increased variety of the quality of sensations changes nothing in the dominating visual scheme. The molecules are invisible, but they move in the same space as the stars, and the physicist does not add anything from his particular observation of matter with other senses than that of sight to the original conception of the astronomer.

Astronomers do not see the movements which they imagine, as these movements are too slow. The physicist similarly does not see the movement of his molecules. He measures an increase in temperature not by his subjective perception of warmth, but by the sight of a thermometer, and he infers that this change is produced by accelerated movements of molecules.

He reduces everything he sees, hears or touches, to the astronomic pattern of bodies moving in space. No amount of physical experience obtained by other senses changes anything in the simple visual scheme based on the movement of the stars.

The only improvement in this conception is the complicated representation of a wave, foreign to astronomy. A single wave is the movement of many millions of particles in a certain regular way, differing from the circular movements of the stars. Both movements have this much in common, that each unit of matter returns periodically to the same position: the planet by revolving round a material centre, the molecule, atom or electron by oscillating around an ideal centre which is on the line of the wave. But, however complicated, this remains still the same movement of bodies of a certain size in space.

The rapid succession of wonderful physical discoveries since 1895, when Lord Rayleigh and Sir

William Ramsay distinguished argon from nitrogen, has changed nothing essential in the physical conception of a molecule. The ingenious methods by which Jean Perrin has shown with astonishing exactness—in his fascinating book *Les Atomes* (Paris, Alcan, 1924)—how many molecules move in a gram of hydrogen, prove only that each molecule occupies a certain space, and within each molecule each atom is also a body of some extension moving in space.

Even the decomposition of atoms, which began in 1898 with the discovery of radium and polonium, only reduced the unit of matter about eighteen hundred times. That ultimate unit, the electron, remains still a body having shape, size, mass, and a rate of speed, like the atoms of a century ago.

Physicists profess to explain the constitution of matter by reducing the size of units and increasing the presumed velocity of movements. But even the smallest body is not simply matter; it is matter having a shape, and this can be distinguished from matter which has taken a different shape.

Physicists are usually unaware of the distinction, and, like astronomers, consider 'bodies in movement' to be sufficient explanation of all material appearances.

We notice the same conservatism in chemistry. The chemist receives from the matter he investigates sensations of smell and taste, but he makes no use of these sensations in the conception he has of matter.

That conception remains the same in chemistry, physics and astronomy. The chemist and the physicist use different senses in their perception of material processes, but they limit themselves to the visual conception of the movement of a body in space when they endeavour to explain what they perceive by other senses.

The imagined movements of molecules, atoms or electrons are essentially of the same quality as the imagined movements of the stars and planets, the only difference being a reduction in size. If we say that a taste or a smell is the result of atomic action on our senses, we simplify and unify the variety of sensations, reducing them all to the visual image of the movement through space with a certain velocity of a body of definite size.

But these quantitative determinations do not explain the qualitative alterations; as, for instance, why chlorine acquires the taste of salt if it is intimately associated with sodium; or why two such gases as hydrogen and nitrogen, which have no smell, combine into ammonia with a pungent odour. Whatever we may imagine about the movements of atoms supplies no explanation of the real chemical changes of which such terms as salts or acids contain a general indication.

We have, however, to accept the qualitative changes acting on smell or taste as primordial facts at least equal in importance to all quantitative determinations,

21

and not to be logically deduced from shape, size, mass and velocity.

Thus it is evident that we utilise for the scientific conception of matter only one of our senses, that of sight. But our sight is by no means the most important of those senses by which we perceive reality. History tells of many sages who were blind, but no deaf man ever became famous for wisdom.

Hearing is more important than sight for acquiring knowledge of reality, because it establishes mutual relations between human individuals, and enables us to compare our sensations and thoughts with those of others.

Acoustics form an important part of physical science, and the study of the waves of sound makes it easier to study the waves of electricity and light. Notwithstanding this, sounds count for nothing in the atomic conception of matter; nor do the sensations of taste, smell or touch, which form such an important part of our sense experience.

This exclusion from the scientific conception of matter of everything that is not some 'body in movement' impoverishes our real knowledge, and creates a chasm between science and common experience. If we wish to judge the quality of a delicious fruit, the best method of investigation is to eat it, and no scientific explanation of the unknown atomic movements which are supposed to produce its taste would give us as much real

22

knowledge of that fruit as mastication, deglutition and digestion.

Nevertheless these experiences are ignored as irrelevant, and naturalists believe themselves to have sufficiently investigated a fruit when they have analysed its anatomic structure and chemical composition and traced its origin.

Thus materialism becomes inconsistent; for if matter is the subject of sensations, we ought to utilise all our sensations, and not only our visual perceptions, in order to understand matter.

Beyond physics and chemistry stands the domain of biology. The biologist, like the chemist, receives many different sensations from the objects of his study; and, like the chemist, he tries to reduce everything to visual images, believing them to afford a sufficient explanation. His favourite instrument is the microscope.

But the living cell differs essentially from the chemical atom and from the physical molecule, as it manifests a continuous flow of assimilation and excretion, unlike concrete bodies in movement.

Organic life produces sensations of taste, smell and touch, not utilised in the metaphysical conception of atomism. Biological realities are translated into visual schemes on the astronomical model: the astronomical tradition has dominated not only physics and chemistry, but biology as well. It is always the image of 'bodies in movement' by

23

means of which biological facts have been represented.

The taste of a fruit, the scent of a flower, the tactile impression of caressing an animal, remain outside the domain of science, and the only reality is held to be the movement of atoms and electrons, similar to that which was first ascribed to the stars, though neither the one nor the other has ever been seen.

In vain does biology reveal to us more and more complex mysteries of organic life. A living cell is by its very nature not an inert 'body in movement'. It has no fixed shape, for life implies a continuous change of size and form. It is not brought into movement by external impulsions, but creates a continuous flow of matter assimilated or excreted.

In this activity finality prevails over the mechanical necessity which is supposed to rule stars or electrons. This predominance of intelligent finality becomes most evident in the last stage of the study of organisms—in mediumistic materialisations as observed by metapsychists within the last fifty years.

Even physicists have been obliged to recognise that these manifestations differ essentially from the supposed movements of stars, molecules, atoms or electrons. It is not any longer a merely quantitative difference of size, shape, mass or velocity, but a really qualitative difference, as between life and death.

A materialisation is not the movement of a body, large or small. Here at last we hit on something totally new that can no longer be explained in the old way. Suddenly there appears a hand, a face, or a complete organism with a beating heart; and as suddenly it disappears.

This teaches us much more about the real essence of the nature of matter than the whole of astronomy, physics, chemistry and biology. These manifestations subserve a purpose which is not a material necessity in the same sense as astronomical, physical or chemical necessities.

Matter acts here on all our senses, but under the influence of an immaterial force. Matter here appears as an instrument of the materialising spirit for the expression of some intellectual or spiritual content. Such matter, obedient to the spirit, could by no means cause or explain the activities of the spirit through movements of invisible bodies in space.

The study of astronomy, of physics, of chemistry, relates to inorganic matter; biology extends the field of enquiry to the organic world, but still remains under the spell of the astronomical tradition; and we had to wait for metapsychics in order to make a new departure in our study of matter.

These experiments furnish the elements of a conception different from the old atomism. The matter of mediumistic materialisations cannot be explained by movements of atoms, after the pattern of the stars. It is matter of a fluid continuity, not to be seized and fixed by sight, as it mocks the senses, suddenly appearing and disappearing in obedience to an immaterial power.

The star, the molecule, the atom, even the electron, are permanent centres which appear to be the elements of manifold combinations. This gross matter dominates and enslaves the spirit, while mediumistic matter is created by the spirit, and is subordinate and obedient to will power.

Thus we see that the succession of sciences leads us beyond materialism and brings us to the conclusion that matter is not a real substance, but something relative and subordinate, dependent on a higher, that is, a spiritual reality.

There were indications of this conclusion as soon as we went beyond the domain of sight, which is the only sense used by the astronomer. Sounds are already something more flexible and fluid than stars or stones. Though translated into waves, the sounds had their own invisible reality of rhythm and measure, quite different from the fixed movements of a revolving star.

The concept of wave, when applied to light and electricity, was so inadequate, that for a long time two competing theories remained in the field. Electric and magnetic phenomena have shown us a form of matter increasingly impalpable in comparison with the blocks of granite of a geologist.

The qualitative transformations due to chemical action were never really accounted for by atomic movements. The process of combustion, which changes hydrogen and oxygen into water, was a qualitative transformation approximating to the elusive matter of the medium. Here something suddenly appeared to the senses out of the invisible.

Biological phenomena were long ago acknowledged to contain more than physics and chemistry could account for, and vitalism tried in vain to satisfy our intellectual craving to understand the difference between life and death, between organic and inorganic matter.

It was reserved for the highest stage of biological research, for metapsychics, to emancipate human intelligence from the naïve representation of 'bodies in movement' as explaining everything material.

We have learnt that bodies may be created by the will of the spirit, and that they disappear as soon as the spirit does not sustain them. This is the most important step since the time of Democritus in the understanding of matter, and leads us to look for other than scientific means in probing the relation of mind to matter.

Science utilises perceptions built out of sensations. These sensations are independent of our will, being given to us as something from without, upon which we have no influence except through experiments, and these of a very limited range.

Thus scientific research deals with matter as it acts on man, and only exceptionally with the reactions of man on matter. There is another vast domain, beyond the range of science, in which from the beginning man dominates and shapes matter. Herein man acts in a totally different way, for instead of observing what already exists, he attempts by his will to transform reality.

He begins where the biologist ends, and his activity raises mankind to a higher level of spiritual achievement than science ever aimed at. That strange magician who starts his career with those materialisations which for the scientist are the latest and most puzzling—is the artist. His purpose is to impress on external matter some form pre-existent in his spirit. He creates matter, or transforms existing matter, according to spiritual needs.

CHAPTER IV

The Matter of Art

Matter for the artist is something other than bodies of definite form moving in space. The artist looks upon matter as formless, even if he uses for his purposes bodies having some elementary form. They are for him merely materials which attain a real and valuable existence only when moulded and upbuilt by art.

We can best judge of the difference between the artist and the scientist if we imagine them both confronted with a block of marble. The scientist will explain the geological origin of the stone, or he will prove that it consists of carbonate of lime by dissolving it in hydrochloric acid, so destroying its structure altogether. The artist will carve a statue out of the shapeless mass, and show what artistic use may be made of this particular kind of stone.

Which of the two will learn more about the intimate nature of marble—the chemist who destroys it and produces invisible carbonic acid out of it, or the sculptor who animates it by giving it a form corresponding to the latent possibilities of that kind of matter? Marble becomes alive in the hands of the sculptor, and is destroyed by the chemist. Which is more important for the human intelligence? to learn of the thousand forms that marble can reveal, or of the few chemical elements contained in it? What shall we say of the chemist who, being offered a delicious peach, instead of eating it, will submit it to chemical analysis? Which of these two men is nearer the truth—the chemist who despises the gourmet for one kind of ignorance, or the gourmet who despises the chemist for another kind of ignorance?

If we wish to understand the nature of marble, is it better to find out how many different forms it can take, and learn of the limitations imposed on the artist by the quality of that kind of matter; to compare the same conception worked out in different materials, and to decide what material best suits a proposed form;—or shall we rather reduce to a chemical formula, or to a geological hypothesis, the quality of the stone, without asking to what use man may put it?

It is evident that in relation to matter of a particular kind, such as marble, every sculptor will be convinced of his superiority over the chemist or the geologist. He will insist upon the obvious truth that only the use of any kind of matter determines its quality for man. We esteem the quality of a peach by the taste, the quality of tea or wine by drinking it, the quality of marble, bronze, ivory, or wood, by admiring the artistic forms which such different materials can take.

The conception of an aim or purpose is more human, and therefore higher than the relation of cause and effect which dominates scientific investigation. Art is creation, while science is only perfected perception of what already exists independently of our consciousness.

Artistic transformation of matter is a higher faculty of the human mind than the theoretic investigation of the chemical and physical interactions of the material world. The most complete knowledge obtained by observation, experiment and thought does not penetrate so intimately the very nature of matter as does an attempt to impress upon relatively shapeless matter a form pre-existing in a creative mind. The growing perfection of forms implies an increasingly close contact between mind and matter, which reveals not only realities but also possibilities undreamt of by the scientist.

In art, as in science, there is a succession of degrees or stages which lead to a closer familiarity of the artist with the matter of his art. But art is much sooner emancipated from the predominance of one sense over others, and this again shows an essential superiority of the artistic attitude over the passive curiosity of the scientist.

Sculpture and architecture are the first stages of art, corresponding to astronomy among the sciences, but using, in addition to sight, the sense of touch and muscular effort. They deal with bodies of rudimentary form, which are heavy to move and remain for ages the same. Sculptors use them to produce and give permanence to visible images, chiefly in imitation of living organisms, gradually rising above mere imitations to a beauty not found in nature.

No human model could inspire Phidias with the divine image of Zeus or Athena. There is in such divine figures a majesty and beauty exceeding anything that can be seen in humanity, and the artist transforms not only a stone into a statue, but also the faces and attitudes of his models into the semblances of gods. If he had not succeeded in making visible what no man had ever seen, he would not have been that immortal artist, admired throughout the centuries.

The architect rises above the sculptor because he uses the work of sculptors to adorn temples or palaces which have no model in nature. A carved god resembles a man more than a temple resembles a cave or a hut in which primitive men have dwelt. An Ionic or Dorian column is more the work of creative imagination, is further removed from the natural tree-forms which led to this architectural conception, than a god-like form is removed from human models.

There is something wonderfully impressive in the permanence of buildings created long ago and outliving their makers by centuries. These buildings do not imitate nature; they serve human purposes, as dwellings or places of worship. In such a building, the stones of which it consists are not all equal to each other like the atoms of Democritus or the electrons of the modern scientists. Each stone has its own place in the whole and is carved according to a plan, as soon as builders outgrow the uniform use of bricks and learn to employ a variety of materials.

This determination of shape by purpose became still more manifest when stones were succeeded by metals and concrete in the latest developments of architecture. In the modern architect's vast constructions of steel and cement the particular shape of each part conforms to a general plan, in striking contrast with the ancient brick buildings, and the architect emancipates himself from many limitations, following his intuitive vision of a reality not revealed to man by nature.

While the sculptor and the architect create permanent forms, the art of dancing consists in the expression of living bodies in ordered movement. Valéry's Platonic dialogue, *L'âme et la danse*, published almost simultaneously (1924) with Havelock Ellis's *The Dance of Life* (1923), demonstrates the sublime dignity of that old art, which has often degenerated into a frivolous and sometimes into an obscene diversion.

Even seventeen centuries ago Plotinus wrote a wonderful passage (*Enneades*, VI, book IX, chap. 9) in which the highest perfection of life is represented as a divine dance. Dancing transforms and glorifies a beautiful human body through rhythmic movement and expression, giving us the true model of 'a body in movement' in a sense superior, through the elements of freedom and ecstasy, to the motions of stars or electrons. Here we witness a double transformation of matter. The appearance of a dancing human body changes continuously, and the body itself changes its position in space. The dancer smiles, bends and sways, fascinating the onlookers by every graceful pose, and moving ever in obedience to a rhythm which is created for the purpose of manifesting fully the beauty of 'the human form divine'.

These three arts—sculpture, architecture, and dancing—show us matter, either static or dynamic, at rest or in movement. To watch the expressive dance of a beautiful body, inspired by a soul attuned to measure and harmony, is an experience in the domain of art which corresponds to the astronomer's contemplation of the slow, precise movement of the stars, with this difference—that the astronomer has no influence at all on the movements he observes, while those who watch a dancer or group of dancers may, to some extent, by manifesting their wishes, change the dance according to their pleasure.

Whether we look at the stars or at the dance, we presume 'bodies in movement'. We see the movement in the dance, but we merely assume it in the stars or electrons. If 'a body in movement' had to

34

become the chief pattern of material reality, it would be the famous and fair Athikte of Valéry's poem, rather than any star, which should reveal to us what 'a body in movement' really is. Her movements are quicker, more unexpected and variable, than the movements of the stars seem to be, for she manifests movement not only in change of place, as do the atom and the star, but also in the change of her expression, her attitudes and gestures, which of course does not happen with atoms or stars.

The real 'body in movement' is not a luminous point; it is a changing artistic shape like that of Athikte, a poet's immortal creation. We should come nearer to absolute reality if, instead of the whirl of dust sung by Lucretius, we took as the original pattern of 'bodies in movement' a well-trained group of beautiful dancers, moving rhythmically in time with a skilled orchestra. We should then notice the wonderful relation between the slight movements of the conductor of the orchestra, the more extended movements of the musicians, and—most expressive of all—those of the dancers.

In the whirls of dust, in the movements of stars, in the nuclei of atoms, we may postulate a conductor who inspires the rhythm, but we cannot see him, and to the senses everything appears to be mere chance or mechanical necessity. There is a revelation of the nature of matter in artistic dance surpassing all the teachings of natural science, because in it we see bodies obeying in their movements a human will. Matter cannot be fully understood without its relation to creative mind, as the very existence of matter is only explicable by the pre-existence of mind and by a finality which remains inexplicable as long as we consider matter apart from mind.

A fourth art leads us still further from the primitive conception of gross matter, though it does not appear to imply any movement. The painter reduces to two dimensions on a plane surface the appearance of three-dimensional objects, and though the picture itself does not move, the objects are often represented as moving, and thus the painter's art is able to produce the illusion of movement. This transformation sublimates matter in a strange way, amounting to a partial dematerialisation of the forms presented to our sight. These forms are animated by colours, which give them the appearance of movement and life to an extent that is scarcely possible in sculpture, and quite impossible in architecture.

The painter uses a variety of colours and shades for his work, while the sculptor and the architect depend usually upon a very limited number of materials. The painter creates new colours by mixing those which exist in nature, and when he tries the effect of a natural pigment, as, for instance, cinnabar, he grasps its true nature more completely than does the chemist who decomposes cinnabar into sulphur and mercury. What the painter knows about cinnabar

36

is much more important for the human mind than what the chemist discovers. The chemist speaks of the elements hidden in cinnabar, but sulphur and mercury are not cinnabar, and there is no explanation of the fact that a silver-grey metallic substance, together with a yellow powder, produces a totally different red substance.

Nor have the other qualities of a compound substance any intelligible relation to the quantities of its components. The chemical composition explains nothing essential. It is only one of many possible relations, and not at all the most important. We cannot even strictly say that cinnabar consists of sulphur and mercury—for we cannot prove the existence of the components in the compound. The real fact is that sulphur and mercury may, under certain conditions, produce cinnabar, but only a painter can show us what various appearances cinnabar can produce in relation to other pigments. Thus he manifests cinnabar as it really is, not split up into parts that bear no resemblance to the whole.

The immediate contrast of many colours in a picture is much more complicated than the form given to a single kind of matter by the sculptor, or to a few kinds of matter by the architect. Painting represents all possible forms imaginable in sculpture, but adds colour and intensifies the impression of movement, so that it helps us to seize the most intimate essence of matter, better than sculpture, architecture or dancing (if we take dancing only as it appears to onlookers, disregarding the muscular sensations of the dancers, which belong to a much more advanced stage of our experience of matter).

Painting also represents wider horizons, a larger part of the material universe, than either sculpture or architecture can display. On a small surface many miles of landscape may be concentrated by the painter, including buildings, some of which may be architectural masterpieces. This power of the painter to condense space raises him above the sculptor, the architect or the dancer, and we conclude that the art of painting is superior to the three preceding arts, as physics and chemistry are superior to astronomy in the knowledge and experience they give of matter.

The process of lifting pictorial art above the function of copying nature, so that it may reveal colours that are rarely seen and forms that never existed, leads us still further in the study of matter to the utmost limit of what sight can reveal about material possibilities.

Painting is apparently able to disregard the very nature of space by representing three dimensions in two, and this is a more thorough transformation, in a sense, than the transformation of qualities in chemical composition. It shows the possibility of a symbolical representation of reality by signs which may be identified by imagination with the objects they depict. The conception of symbolism is not implied in sculpture, nor architecture, nor the dance, as it is in painting. But once acquired it retroacts on all plastic arts, which then appear to be symbolical representations of a thoroughly different reality.

The painter does not pretend to reproduce reality; he represents it in his pictures, which are symbols of reality. Symbolism enters through painting into plastic art, and then reacts on sculpture, the dance, and even architecture. A Gothic cathedral is a symbol of aspiration towards infinity, beyond the limits of Greco-Roman imagination.

Thus from step to step we learn new uses of matter, which reveal new qualities and the possibility of a higher mastery. Above the plastic arts of sculpture and painting rises an art that liberates us totally from bondage to sight and deals with invisible matter. This is the art of music. Sound is material, being the object of sensation. What we hear has the same kind of reality as what we see, and there is no need to reduce to visibility that which strikes our ears immediately in the form of sound. The production of sounds in a certain order, according to the will of the musician, is a use of matter different from that of sculpture and painting: it opens to us the knowledge of a material world without form or colour, yet as real as the world of statues or dancers.

Music reveals a new aspect of matter, not only by its action on the hearers, but also because the musician uses instruments more complicated than

39

those of plastic artists. The manufacture of these instruments is also a plastic activity which imparts definite forms to certain materials, and enables us to study the effect of these forms on the sounds which we wish to produce. Between the simplicity of a painter's or a sculptor's tools and the great complexity of a pianoforte, an organ or a violin there is such an enormous difference that a long succession of experiments in the control of matter by human will was necessary to invent and perfect these instruments. These experiments again brought to light some unexpected qualities in various materials: it was not easy to find out what kind of wood or strings should be used for a perfect violin or piano.

The combination and harmony of many instruments in a modern orchestra correspond to the enormous variety of sounds in this exceedingly complex form of artistic creation. All this human work for artistic and musical purposes was at the same time a study of matter, because the manufacture of instruments added much to our knowledge of the materials that were used. This plastic activity of the manufacturers of instruments was supplementary to the efforts of the composers and performers, who by a succession of sounds contrived to express immaterial realities, namely emotions and inspirations.

Here, as in metapsychics, matter appears as a tool of the spirit, and ceases to be a self-existing power independent of man, such as is the matter dealt with by astronomers, physicists, chemists, geologists and biologists. The metapsychical experience consisting in the materialisation of something invisible and impalpable is repeated at a higher level in musical art. Music materialises a spiritual reality, for the succession and harmony of sounds has a peculiar relation to the infinite variety of emotions and inspirations, which in their ultimate stage produce mystical ecstasy. A life very much superior to the life of the senses is revealed here through sensations.

At a lower level sensation enslaves the sensuous man, but for the artist it is subordinated to the spirit, and expresses realities of a nature far superior to matter, strangely enough through material means. It is a sublimation of that life of feeling which in the beginning was common to men and animals. The knowledge of matter won in this way reveals mysteries which are not expressed by plastic artists or by scientists.

Chopin teaches a musical mind more about the relation between soul and body, between matter and spirit, than the most marvellous discoverer in biology or even metapsychics. Supreme musical artists, such as Paderewski, awake an immediate response in the masses such as no sculptor or painter, nor even perhaps an exquisite dancer, could hope to gain. Musicians travel over land and sea with their intricate instruments and are worshipped almost as gods, earning applause and material rewards such as no scientist nor any plastic artist ever received.

But the meaning of melodies and symphonies remains ambiguous, and may be interpreted in different ways, so that there is in music a yearning for an even more adequate expression of mental contents. Such a tendency finds satisfaction in a higher art, which expresses not only emotions, but also thoughts and actions, through words, rhymes and rhythms. This is the art of poetry, which deals with a matter still subtler than that of sounds, as it consists in words and rhythms which do not even need to be uttered aloud to reveal their beauty, provided that they are clearly imagined.

Words are the matter of poetry. Words may be thought or imagined in connection with one another, without being spoken. An unspoken verse is a verse made of unspoken words, and may amount to a wonderful creation before anybody has heard or appreciated it. If such verses are pronounced, a musical impression is added, which is not, however, indispensable to the poetic purpose. Words are matter of a kind that is invisible, impalpable, beyond the reach of the senses. Still they are matter, because they can be used by the poet as material for rhymes, rhythms and verses. Poetical art produces material-isations of spiritual beauty just as do music, painting and the plastic arts.

Poetry gives form to the material of words and

sentences; thus the poet may be called a plastic artist as is the sculptor, the painter, the musician; but the matter which he uses can be controlled by the mind without affecting the senses. It is sufficient to think the words in a certain order: thereby we express what is intended and create a work of art. We may then pronounce or write the verses which the poet has made, but they were already made when he thought them, as a beautiful verse possesses all its beauty before it has been uttered, written or printed.

The unspoken poem has a similar relation to the sound of the same poem when it is uttered, as the two-dimensional image of the painter to the same object carved by the sculptor. An unspoken poem is a reality of which the sound of the words is a symbol. Yet the unspoken word is a kind of matter, because it can serve the purpose of building a verse or a poem, as a brick serves the purpose of building a house.

The words of languages have a certain kind of symbolical existence in dictionaries, but they have existed in minds before they were included in dictionaries. Though they do not directly strike our eyes or ears, we think them as sounds and we hear them inwardly, so that we may say that an unspoken verse is perceived as something material, a construction of the matter of words.

It is not easy to understand that words are a kind of matter, but so long as we do not extend our conception of matter so far as to include the words of a language, we remain unable to fathom the magnificent variety of material phenomena.

In speaking, writing or printing his verses, the poet shares with others his own intimate spiritual experience, and in doing so makes an objective use of the words of his language, modifying, more or less, their meaning in the minds of his hearers or readers. Sometimes he creates new words, new modes of expression, new ways of using words, and then he creates matter that has not existed before, in a sense in which almost every artist is able to create the matter of his art.

In poetry we witness the real creation of matter by the spirit in a sense still deeper than that in which we speak of the creation of sounds by the musician, or of new shades of colour by the painter. What we say of unspoken poems is also true of melodies in the mind of the musician, pictures in the mind of the painter, sculptures in the mind of the sculptor, before these artistic conceptions have been given an outward objective appearance. But a verse created by a poet has greater precision than any image or statue imagined by a painter or sculptor. A verse consists of definite words, and can be repeated many times without any alteration. The poet remembers his creation when he speaks or writes his poem, and he knows that nothing has been lost.

This is not the case with painters or sculptors who cannot exactly compare their finished works with their first inspiration. Therefore the reality and objectivity of the unspoken poem is superior to that of the unpainted picture existing in the painter's mind. The unwritten music existing in the musician's soul may approach the precision of unspoken verses, but perfect memory of musical sounds seems to be a rarer gift than perfect memory of words and sentences.

Even a sound consists of matter subtler than a star or an electron. But the word is subtler still, and more subordinated to the spirit, for it needs no instrument to serve the poet's purpose. Accordingly, as we rise from one stage to another in the hierarchy of arts, we notice an increasing predominance of spirit over matter. The sculptor or the architect depends more on the matter of his art than the painter or dancer. The painter depends more on the matter of his art than the musician, because he mostly imitates models, while the musician creates them. The poet achieves the greatest freedom among artists and reaches the utmost limits of creative art, for he gives life to what has never existed.

Finally—there is a supreme art, superior even to pure poetry, because it is the final synthesis of all preceding arts, the living representation of an aspect of human life. Its matter is dramatic poetry with every kind of decoration furnished by sculpture, architecture and painting, sometimes combined with music, song and dance. This is the theatrical art,

45

which must be distinguished from the mere staging of a dramatic work, and here the poet's text constitutes the matter, to which very much must be added in order to create a successful performance.

We speak therefore of the *creation* of Shakespeare's *Hamlet* by a gifted actor; for instance, by Sir Henry Irving. Shakespeare imagined the character of Hamlet, as expressed in the words of the text. Sir Henry Irving added the intonation, the gestures, the movements, and this is the highest art, as it gives form to matter of the subtlest kind. The producer may see in a dramatic work more than the poet himself could see. Sometimes the poet does not fully appreciate his own inspiration: the stage is the final test for the work of the dramatic poet.

A producer of plays uses all the existing means to express human life, which, as a spiritual reality, is essentially immaterial. In the theatre we have to compare three different points of view which mutually supplement one another:

(1) We have first the *author's* vision of an aspect of human life which he endeavoured to represent by means of words and sentences.

(2) Then comes a *producer*, who should himself be a perfect actor, inspiring other actors and showing them how each part should be played, as is done by the famous Juljusz Osterwa, director of the Polish National Theatre called *Reduta*. Interpretations of a play may amount to a new creation of beauty undreamt-of by the author.

(3) Finally, there is the *audience* which appreciates or rejects that interpretation. The sympathy of the audience exalts the creative faculties of the actors, decorators, dancers and musicians.

The author furnishes the matter, but it is the producer and the actors who give to that matter a form which can fully satisfy and enthral an audience. Such a perfect representation of an inspired play, under the guidance of one who is himself a poet and actor of genius, furnishes exceptional opportunities for reflecting on the relation between the stage and life, between matter and spirit. The rehearsal of a play is a test of integral art, with the utilisation of all special arts, in order to create the fittest expression of an aspect of life. The aim of the theatrical art is to lead us out of our ordinary lives and to initiate us into the life of others as represented on the stage. This stage-life is the artistic condensation of human experience, derived from the actual lives of those who portray the characters represented.

Whoever has not learnt to enjoy a good theatrical performance knows real life only from his own narrow experience. It is art alone that gives to matter the various forms by means of which the accumulated life-experience of many generations may be expressed. These attempts reveal the possibilities of a material representation of life through the combination of all arts on the stage, and they give therefore many opportunities for a deeper understanding of matter.

Thus art penetrates the mystery of matter more completely than science, the various sciences and arts forming an ascending scale of more and more intimate apprehension of its nature. The growing knowledge of the true nature of matter leads us at the same time to a deeper understanding of spirit, as we see that the more we advance in our intimate knowledge of matter through the sciences and arts, the more it becomes evident that matter depends on spirit and exists only in relation to spirit.

The matter of metapsychics is subtler, less overwhelming, than the matter of geology or astronomy. The verse of the poet, the gesture and intonation of the actor, the setting of the producer, deal with matter still subtler, still more obedient to human will, than the stone of the sculptor or the colours of the painter.

There is a certain analogy between the progressive succession of sciences and the evolution of art, which leads up to an ideal representation of spiritual reality through material appearances created and transformed by the artist's will. The work of the artist is a fit supplement to the investigations of the scientist. Both help us towards the final solution of the mystery of matter; but there are still other human activities which, having distinct aims, contribute to the mastery of matter by spirit, and therefore also to a deeper knowledge of what matter really is.

CHAPTER V

Business

Besides the love of knowledge and the need of beauty there is a third motive for efforts leading to the mastery of matter by the spirit. This third aim is general usefulness, the satisfaction of human needs by the skilled distribution of the products of labour. These activities relate to matter, transform and shape matter, and furnish new experiences as to the nature of matter.

In the world of business both science and art are utilised for purposes of usefulness and for the creation of wealth. Wealth secures leisure, and leisure is the condition alike of scientific research and of artistic creation. Thus business on one side utilises sciences and arts, and on the other side foments their growth.

The final mastery of the bulk of matter on earth could never have been achieved by the fine arts, which always deal with insignificant quantities of matter. This final mastery is the task of business in its widest aspect, beginning with hunting, fishing and primitive housekeeping, and ascending gradually to the highest practical activities.

We notice in business, as in science and art,

successive degrees of initiation into an increasingly complete mastery of the material world. Those who fish or hunt, kill animals for food and very soon learn the most elementary transformation of food by cooking. Between the living animal escaping pursuit and the cooked meat of the same animal there are instructive qualitative differences.

The living animal is perceived by sight, hearing and smell—a much more real 'body in movement' than either star or electron. The meat of the killed animal furnishes sensations of taste, smell and touch, as well as those of sight. This is the most familiar experience of a transformation of matter. Fishermen and hunters become acquainted with nature: they experience the changes of weather—storms, floods, fires—and they try to explain material phenomena by the action of spirits; but they have to take nature as it is and cannot dream of influencing what goes on around them. The reality of events overwhelms them, and incites them to worship the power of the gods of nature, whom they suppose to rule their lives.

A totally different human attitude towards the material world arises when man learns to domesticate wild animals. The wandering pastoral tribes feed their herds on the natural growth of grass and foliage. But at a higher stage they learn to till the soil, to sow and reap, and to remain settled on the ground they have cultivated.

Agriculture is a higher activity than fishing and

hunting, even as painting rises above sculpture. The cultivation of the soil and the breeding of domestic animals initiates us into the mysteries of influencing natural processes so as to produce entirely new kinds of organisms. The grass of natural prairies is changed into corn, the wolves into various kinds of dogs, the tigers and lions into cats. We have here on an immense scale a humanisation of nature according to our needs and tastes. The relation of man to domestic animals implies a certain modification of that brutality which is generally to be expected from those who merely capture them for food. Agriculture is intended gradually to transform the whole surface of the earth, and this tendency is seen to reach its highest stage in horticulture, with its intensive cultivation of flowers and fruits.

As the human population grows denser, we notice a natural transition from animal food to vegetarianism or fruitarianism, and a lively interest in the prevention of cruelty to animals. The business of food and clothing for man is carried on with an increasing mastery of natural conditions.

This emancipation of the human spirit from nature goes on also in the workshops in which craftsmen devise various means for utilising natural or artificial fabrics for human needs of clothing, footgear and all kinds of implements. The craftsmen work individually, chiefly with their hands and certain tools. But invention of more complicated tools leads to the introduction of machinery, which reduces muscular effort and accelerates production.

Thus we witness the introduction into human life of modern industry, which shapes matter on an unprecedented scale over the whole surface of the earth, and modifies the natural conditions of human life in the sense of lessening physical effort and increasing the proportionate results of our slightest muscular movements.

Decisive steps in this progress are: the invention of motors; the substitution of exploding gases for the pressure of steam; the utilisation of water levels and tides and of differences of temperature between different depths in the sea; the exploitation of wind power and all kinds of natural forces many times stronger than our muscles.

This control of nature teaches us the power of the spirit over material appearances, and liberates us from constant anxiety concerning elementary needs. In this respect modern industry rises above agriculture, as music above painting. It creates greater wealth and more leisure than could ever be achieved by pastoral or agricultural populations.

If we compare the old guns used a few generations ago with a modern browning, we see how the famous bow of Odysseus has been improved in every respect. The rapidity and efficiency of action has grown enormously, while the size of the weapon has been reduced. The same has happened with other instruments. The production of a steel nib, a fountain-pen, or a typewriter, compared with the cutting of the old-fashioned quill, is a familiar example of the great simplification of use resulting from an enormous complication of the method of manufacture.

The most conspicuous result of this mastery of will and imagination over matter is the improvement of the means of communication between distant places. The introduction of the steam railway seemed to be a definitive achievement, but the electrification of railways, and the invention and gradual perfecting of airways, have greatly increased the speed and comfort of travelling. This amounts to an essential alteration in our conception of space. The possibility of crossing from Europe to America in a week would have been incredible to our ancestors. Now we are almost in sight of accomplishing such a voyage in one or two days.

The transmission of news by mail, by telegraph, telephone and radio, unifies mankind to an unprecedented extent. This shows how technical inventions influence intellectual and even spiritual life. But far more important is the growing power of human will over the material world through a succession of increasingly efficient tools. Matter ceases to limit our efforts as was the case with primitive man. The effect of civilisation is to subordinate matter to man.

Commercial activity has been parallel to industrial production. The goods produced had to be brought

53

to the consumer, and the distribution all over the earth of the products of industry challenged the resources of the human mind to no less an extent than the invention of machinery. The machinery of international commerce and credit is not less ingenious than the machinery of industrial production. And at the top we find the banking system, enabling everybody to dispense his means in the quickest and simplest way.

We are no longer burdened by having to carry coins with which to pay for all our acquisitions. A cheque payable in London can be cashed anywhere. Banknotes enable us to carry a fortune in our pockets. Hence a symbol representing value acquires real value. There is scarcely any industrial transformation so stupendous as the fact that a mere signature can change a worthless piece of paper into the equivalent of a million pounds, for which vast real estate—houses, shops, ships—may be bought without our moving from the office in which such transactions are completed.

There is a skill in these transactions which may increase not only the wealth of a successful business man, but the general wealth of mankind, for the value of products depends very much on the place in which they are available, so that skilful distribution arranged by commercial correspondence increases the value of stocks. The centralisation of markets on the whole reduces the price of commodities for the consumer.

In earlier centuries it might happen that the same gold coin would secure a hundred times more eggs in Russia than in England. Now the London market price is wired all over Europe every day, and regulates the purchases for the producers and consumers in most countries. Such achievements of international business are of the utmost importance for the realisation of lasting peace between nations, and for the harmony of all classes collaborating in the efforts which lead to an increasing liberty in the pursuit of intellectual and artistic aims.

There are still other fields of business besides agriculture, industry, commerce and banking. Lawyers do business in connection with the production and distribution of wealth. Physicians use the theoretical knowledge of physiology and pathology in healing the sick, and they gain a peculiar practical experience of matter which the theoretic study alone could not give. Soldiers use scientific knowledge and technical skill for the defence of goods produced by industry and disposed of by commerce.

The business of war, of law, of medicine increases our knowledge of matter, because it deals chiefly with material values to be preserved or increased. Health, economic justice, safety from enemies, have a material value and are matter of business. We might question whether the clergyman could be named along with the engineer, the agriculturalist, the banker, the lawyer, the physician and the soldier, as belonging to

55

the same world of business, distinct from the worlds of science and art.

In the spiritually perfect society, called *the Kingdom of God*, there will be no room for lawyers, nor for soldiers, nor for physicians—and clergymen will also become superfluous. But in our imperfect life we need clergymen as teachers and helpers, whose influence—apart from their religious duties—tends to limit competition among people engaged in business, and to encourage whole-hearted co-operation. Therefore as long as lay people need the help of the clergy in their practical pursuits, we must acknowledge that the clergyman belongs to the same professional class as the lawyer, the physician and the soldier, whose work is subsidiary to the production and distribution of wealth. The clergyman's business is to teach and to advise, to prevent such wrongs as the lawyer cannot avert, and to change the hearts of the wrong-doers so that they may offer reparation to their victims. We may consider the clergyman as a kind of spiritual lawyer, improving the general atmosphere of the world of business.

The life of business, being based on science and art, supplements them in a way distinct from intellectual and artistic activity. The wish to create material values penetrates the material world in a very peculiar manner and the business man observes such aspects of matter as neither the scientist nor the artist is concerned with.

If we go back to the example of the different attitude of a scientist and a sculptor towards a block of marble, we shall easily see what the attitude of the business man will be. He will enquire where more of this artistically useful material can be found, will buy the quarries, organise workmen to extract the valuable stone, and distribute blocks of convenient size to sculptors living in many cities. Marble in the quarry has little value, but when brought to the right place and to the right artists it becomes material for valuable masterpieces.

Such a business man renders service and acquires personal wealth, but obviously he also increases enormously the value of the wares he handles. He gives employment to his workmen, profits to railway companies, and artistic enjoyment to those who contemplate the work of sculptors. Thus the business man makes many people work and enables them to satisfy their needs.

The talent for industrial and commercial organisation differs from scientific or artistic capacity; for while the scientist or the artist works in isolation, the business man, the organiser of agriculture, industry or commerce combines the efforts of others towards the fulfilment of social purposes. The matter of the business man consists of living men, including scientists and artists. He makes them work for definite purposes, with the general aim of improving human life by increasing facilities for satisfying material needs, whereby the obstacles to a fullness of intellectual, artistic and spiritual endeavour are removed.

The scientist satisfies in the first place his own intellectual curiosity, but serves society incidentally thereby; the artist creates beauty first of all for his own enjoyment, awakening appreciation of its mystery in others almost involuntarily. But the business man, even if personal wealth is his chief object, has to consider others at every step of his efforts. Thus the business man acts for the common good of his neighbours if he clearly understands the close connection between his own advantage and his general usefulness.

The full development of business activity comes later in the life of mankind than that of science and art, and requires the utilisation of all scientific and artistic resources. Therefore we must recognise business as a third way leading to a deeper understanding of matter, and the matter of business is the desires and needs of men, a still subtler reality than the unuttered word of the poet. At the same time the man of business also deals with every kind of matter acted on by scientists and artists. In business there is a synthesis of the intellectual achievement of science with the artistic realisation of beauty.

There is a sphere of business beyond the work of all those professional experts whom we have mentioned. It is the political business of government, which has as its matter the state, and as its chief purpose the realisation of justice in the personal relations between citizens. At a lower stage men of business struggle against each other, and this competition threatens the welfare of society. It is the business of the true statesman to transform competition into harmonious co-operation, and to secure an equitable distribution of the advantages resulting from human endeavour.

This is the highest achievement in the world of business, like theatrical art among the arts. State government co-ordinates all human efforts towards one goal—the perfection of life. For the business of government all citizens of a state become the matter of a final structure, a happy and peaceful commonwealth. The real matter of this business consists of the hopes and aspirations, the fears and hates, of men. It is the true statesman's business to raise these aspirations, fulfil these hopes, and allay these fears and hates.

CHAPTER VI

Training and Sexual Life

Science, art and business are not the only avenues through which man gains experience of matter. They all deal with external matter, which is naturally independent of us. In science we seek to perceive and to understand what this matter is; in art we endeavour to mould it and thus to transform it; in business we use the resources of science and art in order to satisfy our material needs or to safeguard our material productions.

In all these cases we deal by means of our body with something that is outside our body. But our body is also material, and it is the source of sensations much keener than those which come from without. Sexual enjoyment, from the material standpoint, is a sensation, no less than headache, indigestion, heart palpitation, fatigue, exhaustion, hunger, thirst and even death.

The power of controlling physical sensations belongs neither to science, nor to art, nor to business, but to a fourth great human activity, which in its negative aspect is usually called *asceticism*, but may be generally designated as the training of body and mind.

Many men submit to every craving of the body without any attempt at controlling their senses. A long succession of experiences met by sustained efforts in self-government is needed to emancipate such slaves. But it is not the scientist, the artist, or the man of business who best succeeds in subjugating the animal in man. There is a fourth kind of expert, totally different from these, who struggles with his body in order to conquer it, namely the *ascetic*.

The elementary stage of asceticism is a negative discipline, consisting in the elimination from life of every fleshly indulgence. The typical ascetic limits sleep and food, wears hair shirts, inflicts on himself pains of every kind, remains for long hours without movement, keeps protracted silence, and generally deprives himself of everything pleasurable.

He learns in these exercises to renounce many things which seem to most men indispensable. He treats the matter of his body as an enemy, and this matter is no longer a shape, or a colour, or a sound; it is not even an unuttered word; it represents to him what is called *temptation*.

Temptation acts on the senses, and is an object of sensuous craving; therefore it is matter, as truly as stones and shapes and colours and sounds and words. But if some people find a difficulty in realising that unspoken words may also be matter, it will seem to the majority almost incredible that what we call 'temptation' should be identified with matter, that eternal adversary of the spirit which is only partly controlled by art and business. Yet there is no final understanding of what matter really is without this last step of recognising in the ascetic striving to conquer the temptations of the flesh as worthy an effort to solve the mystery of matter as we have seen in the scientist, the artist and the man of business.

Temptation consists in every sensuous craving which confronts the will of the ascetic. It may be the desire for a particular food or drink, or for the touch of a person of the other sex. It is not a visible or palpable shape, nor an invisible sound, nor an unpronounced word, but it is as real as any of these, though existing only in the imagination, as do the words in our thought before they are uttered.

A temptation to which the ascetic does not yield is like an unspoken word, and quite as material, since it acts on the senses. The temptation of the ascetic is matter even subtler than the unspoken word of the poet; yet it has a tremendous material power which threatens the spirit with extinction.

The aim of the ascetic is to control that matter by completely annihilating it. If he yields, he creates new matter that has not existed before, as every temptation to which he falls victim produces a long chain of others which could have been prevented, had the first temptation been overcome when it arose in the mind.

Every temptation conquered increases our power over our body, every temptation yielded to lessens it and enslaves us yet more. Thus the struggle against temptations is a training of will power, which gives us mastery over our own body. This negative discipline consists chiefly in limiting food and sleep, abstaining from sexual indulgence and from every superfluous action, especially from idle words.

The temptation to indulge in speech which may pain or injure others is sometimes a temptation more obstinate and more difficult to overcome than the coarser temptations of the flesh. Cruel or unjust speech is a manifestation of pride, the source of many sins.

More important than all negative mortification, we have to recognise a positive discipline as leading equally to the control of the body and to the elimination of temptations. While negative discipline weakens the body in order to conquer it more easily, positive training strengthens and beautifies it through graceful movement, appropriate diet and careful hygiene. This is the domain of gymnastics, including respiratory exercises, all kinds of sports and games, and also that perfect art of the dance, imagined by Valéry, from the point of view of the participator, not merely from that of the spectator.

Positive training, if it builds up a body healthy, strong, beautiful, chaste, skilled, and controlled by the will, penetrates more deeply into the mystery of matter than negative asceticism, which conquers a body weak and well-nigh exhausted. Positive training of the body destroys temptations no less effectively than starvation and self-inflicted tortures.

Training in general consists in the periodical repetition of positive or negative acts of will, in relation to our body, with the purpose of developing and transforming that body. In such discipline it is found to be a rule that every successful effort lessens the difficulty of ensuing efforts, until we achieve the most difficult things without strain.

The full perfection of activity is reached when there is no painful struggle, and this is the ultimate outcome of a long, regular training. We learn thus to limit or to intensify our movements at will, and to do exactly what we consider right, neither more nor less. Ambition, such as that of the ordinary sportsman to beat previous records, is not in the line of genuine training. The perfection of movements is not a quantitative determination, but a qualitative one. It does not matter whether a disc is thrown a greater distance than ever before if such an effort destroys the beauty of the movement. The supreme achievement of training is to conceal the efforts which have led to a particular result.

Thus training initiates us into an aspect of the relation between body and soul, or matter and spirit, which neither science, nor art, nor business could reveal. It is our own body, a materialisation of our soul, which we develop and transform by training.

This is the kind of matter which we know best, and which is most intimately associated with our soul.

The outcome of training is a peculiar mastery of the spirit over matter, distinct from the achievements of art or business. Our body is material, but it is connected with our soul in a very special way, so that its influence over our soul is greater than that of any other material object. If matter in general is opposed to spirit, if there is in the universe a struggle between matter and spirit, that struggle has to be fought out definitively in every individual body animated by an incarnated spirit.

The mastery of external matter becomes possible only through the control of our own body, and this requires alternately negative asceticism and positive training. Thus training, in the widest sense of that term, becomes a fourth way, in addition to those of science, art and business, leading to the knowledge of matter.

There is one kind of training in which the control over our own body is intimately associated with a very strange relation to another body, a relation which is simultaneously active and passive, because mutual. This is the experience of sexual life,[1] the

[1] The whole problem of sexual life and of the final aim of sexuality is treated more amply in the author's *World of Souls* (pp. 196–220) in chapter VII: 'A new theory of sex'. There also the mystery of conception is explained as a spiritual reality, and a possible conciliation between the classic and the romantic view of love and marriage is attempted.

close connection of two persons of different sex in which bodies and souls are implicated, so that a predominance of the body in one of the partners threatens the other with a similar defeat, while the mastery of one soul over its body has an equally reciprocal effect.

The difference between the sexes creates special temptations, which it is easier to avoid by running away from them than by bravely facing them, and transforming them through the sublimation of passion. Conjugal chastity is more difficult than monastic chastity, and teaches us more about the nature of our bodies. The union of two who truly love can take place without any consciousness of sin, and remain not only joyous but also pure. Impurity is in our conscience, and the verdict of our conscience is not arbitrary, as it does not depend on our desires. If our conscience does not reproach us for an act which might be condemned in others, then the particular act in question really belongs to a different class, whatever its outward appearance. Sexual union then becomes a mystic ecstasy, in which the lovers are almost unaware of their bodies, and then their union differs inwardly from what it might appear to outsiders to be. In such cases the lovers themselves are the most reliable witnesses of their own experience and not those who judge them from the outside, without being able to grasp the true reality of their common inspiration. But those who yield to impure temptations—whether in the married or unmarried state—and who involuntarily give life to bodies tainted with the heredity of uncontrolled passion, are unable to conceive the ecstasy of a voluntary pro-creation of pure new bodies, which may become, through prayer and self-dedication, a sacramental act.

Carnal passion is the violent craving for sensual satisfaction, while the very existence of the body may be disregarded when two lovers are united in a joint prayer for worthy and noble offspring—in an un-selfish dedication of two lives that a third life may ensue, in conformity with the will of God.

Voluntary procreation in a conjugal union thus consecrated is the highest form of materialisation, consisting of the offering of new living bodies to souls of the purest nature. It teaches us more about the essence of matter than any other kind of negative or positive training.

Sexual life, the closest intimacy of two persons of different sex, reveals certain new aspects of the relation between body and mind, and manifests either the superiority of will and mind over the body, or the degradation of the soul. This peculiar type of positive training leads to an emancipation from the yoke of the senses, such as cannot be achieved by the mere avoiding of opportunities of contact. The transformation and sublimation of physical desire into the spiritual rapture of a marriage of the highest type conceivable, in which the real and sincere motive

67   5-2

is the humble and loving offering of a body to a discarnate spirit, leads to the liberation of mankind from the tragic consequences of that terrible prehistoric catastrophe, known as the Fall, or Original Sin.

However, if we admit that incarnation is not merely an accidental and exceptional state for a spirit, but the normal recurrence of a natural condition suitable for its growth, then it follows that other aspects of sexual life, besides perfect union, must be a part of the age-long training of the soul.

One of these aspects is monastic seclusion, which isolates one sex from the other. Such an isolation retains its sexual character, though it excludes intercourse. If sexual temptations were not so strong, the recourse to monasteries would never have been thought of. The monk among monks remains a man; the nun among nuns remains a woman; and one sex deprived of intercourse with the other sex still affirms its sexuality.

Between the negative discipline of celibacy and the perfect union of pure love there are many stages, and every individual soul has its own sexual experiences in a long succession of lives. The presence as well as the absence of the other sex belongs to the general domain of sexual life, as long as sex distinction exists among mankind. In each life some aspect of this reality is experienced, and the higher stages presuppose the lower in long-forgotten lives.

Thus, the training of individuals and of couples repeats the lesson of science, art and business, by showing us again the relativity of matter, and leading to a liberation and emancipation of the spirit. We may now ask whether there is an activity which supplements training, in a way similar to that in which science supplements art. Science is passive. Art is active. Science observes, calculates, predicts. Art transforms matter, gives shape to matter, and even creates it. If training acts positively on the body, transforms, perfects and sanctifies the body, what will be the corresponding domain of a similar but passive process? We call it ritual, manifested in the cult or worship of material objects which are held to be the foci for the concentration of spiritual powers.

CHAPTER VII

Ritual

Matter may become in certain exceptional circumstances a receptacle for spiritual force, if we accept the authority of certain men of the widest experience who have introduced a peculiar use of material things into the ritual of the religious life. From the remotest ages we find faith in the mysterious powers of relics or talismans among all peoples. A relic or talisman is a material object supposed to be impregnated with subtle force by a powerful spirit.

There are not only religious, but also national or personal, relics. The pen of a great writer, the sword of a famous conqueror, may be held in reverential awe like the bones of a saint. In all such cases it is supposed that matter which has for long been in contact with a great spirit retains something of the power of that spirit.

Thus, some people are fain to believe that a pen which in the hand of a genius has served to write masterpieces may help an inferior writer to rise above his own natural level. This presupposes a concentration of purely spiritual forces in a material object.

It may appear at first sight to involve a somewhat materialistic conception of a spiritual force, acting like the electric current which transforms iron into a magnet. But if spirit acts on matter, and matter reacts on spirit, we may easily conceive that action corresponds to reaction in such a way that matter rendered thoroughly submissive to a powerful spirit becomes thereby able to transmit the power received to other spirits, just as a vanquished enemy may be incorporated into the army of the conqueror.

This would not at all mean a materialistic conception of spiritual power, but quite the reverse; i.e. the annihilation of material resistance, so that matter becomes spiritualised. In the eternal warfare between matter and spirit, spiritual beings are sometimes dominated by their bodies, but it is also possible for material bodies to be deprived of their recalcitrance and completely dominated by the spirit for an indefinite period.

This indicates a final capitulation of matter and the definitive triumph of spirit. In art, in business, in training we have observed always a certain quality of resistance in matter, and efforts were needed to overcome it partially and temporarily. A relic is matter lastingly impregnated by spirit, and consequently losing its material character and becoming itself a source of spiritual efficacy.

Faith in relics is almost universal and has wide applications. A relic may be not only a small material object, but an article of furniture, or a building in which spiritual forces were once active. The walls of a church may be influenced by the prayers of bygone generations in such a way that they afford inspiration to later worshippers. The pulpits from which famous sermons have been preached may help to kindle the eloquence of the young preacher of a succeeding age.

Not only do good influences thus impregnate matter, but also evil thoughts and feelings. The walls of a gambling den may incite men to risk all they possess in a mad challenge to fate. The boudoir of a great courtesan may awaken or stimulate voluptuous desires, even in innocent persons, unaware of the associations of such a place. Houses of Parliament incite to idle talk and stupid party strife. The Reading Room of the British Museum creates an atmosphere of study, and may inspire the ingenious interpretation of difficult texts.

Thus we constantly create relics by our attitude of mind. The essential passivity of matter is impregnated by the fundamental activity of spirit, for good or evil, without our awareness of the magic force we exercise, save in exceptional cases.

A wedding ring is a talisman supposed to be impregnated with the force of the solemn vows made by husband and wife, and may help in conquering temptations to break such vows. A seal is not only the sign of a pact, but also a help towards the fulfilment of accepted obligations. A whole city, Jerusalem, has been sanctified by the Crucifixion of the Saviour. Another city, Rome, the cradle of civil and ecclesiastical law, had become personified as the very Spirit of Law.

In all these cases popular opinion supposes spiritual force to be fixed in matter. Matter acquires here a new aspect, never suspected by science, art, business or training. It has resisted the efforts of the scientist, the artist, the man of business, the ascetic. We are accustomed to distinguish matter from spirit as an adverse force. The faith in relics, which is instinctive, even in many irreligious men, suggests the contrary possibility—that matter may become a positive auxiliary of spirit. The bones of a saint are supposed to work miracles similar to those that the saint himself might have worked.

At first sight this may appear to be a superstition devoid of any foundation. But in the light of the whole succession of efforts in art, business and asceticism to conquer matter, the conclusion that matter may be finally conquered and utilised for spiritual aims is seen as a natural outcome of all the preceding stages. We have remarked in art the growing mastery of spirit, and the gradual de-materialisation of matter, until it became an inward reality in thought or imagination without outward manifestation. In business, matter gradually became the invisible reality of credit, invoked by a signature. In asceticism and positive training, the body grew more and more to be the expression and instrument

73

of the soul. Why should all this age-long struggle not lead to a final victory?

Already, in metapsychics and asceticism, the body seems to be partially annihilated, as, for instance, when it is levitated in defiance of gravitation, or when it is kept alive for long periods without food.

When material relics are charged with spiritual power, the last stage of that process is reached. Matter naturally depends upon spirit and it was intended by the Creator to serve spiritual ends. It was, according to the oldest traditions, the creature that rebelled against its Creator; first the angels and then men, tempted by a fallen angel.

Gradually the material world is being redeemed and made a vehicle of spiritual power. The use of matter in religious ritual is the sixth great way of initiation into these mysteries, after science, art, business, sexual life and training. Science, sexuality and worship are passive; art, business and training, active. There is an analogy between the relations of art to science and training to worship. Training makes the body a vehicle for spiritual forces; worship perceives and reverences the radiance and power of existing relics.

These exceptional cases in which relics are recognised and worshipped lead us to a more general induction as to the mutual relations of matter and spirit in the universe. That power which becomes manifest in the relic of a Saint may also act when unnoticed and unrecognised; thus each soul is continuously transforming its material environment for good or for evil.

In addition to all the material processes subject to our observation, there has been, since the very beginning, a constant action of spirit on matter taking place everywhere, and slowly transforming the material universe. Conversely, matter acts on spirit as a hindrance and limitation.

In this struggle we behold the final victory of spirit as manifested in genuine relics of saints. The creation of matter was an effect of the Fall, and the sanctification of the spirit reacts on the material universe by means of dematerialisation. This is a general process for ever at work throughout the universe, and not merely an exceptional occurrence, as is supposed by the worshippers of particular relics. We learn from them that spirit may sanctify matter, but we have to extend this operation over the whole material universe. This may be done through the close association of human beings in religious worship and national aspiration.

The belief in the possibility of concentrating spiritual powers in material objects finds its most thorough application in the Catholic doctrine of the sacraments. A sacrament is a visible sign of invisible grace. It is a kind of matter that is even more completely controlled by spirit than the body of the ascetic or the athlete, because the matter of sacraments is not subject to temptations, and has a power that cannot be lost.

This sacramental power is transmitted by means of an action different from that of the scientist, the man of business, the lover, the artist, or the ascetic; and the function of matter in the sacraments is far superior to that seen in science, art, love, business or asceticism. A sacrament is a relic created by the faith, prayer and act of will of an expert, specially trained by the exercises of the priesthood.

The effect of sacramental consecration in the sacrament of the Eucharist is called *transubstantiation*. According to Catholic doctrine the change is not observable from without—it is concealed within the unchanged outward appearances. This is just what happens with every relic. A sword worn and used by a great conqueror does not change to outward observation. The courage, prudence and wisdom of the owner are supposed to act in it mysteriously so as to produce courage, prudence and wisdom in others who may wear and use the same weapon.

Materialists will deny the possibility of such a supernatural power in relics and sacraments. But those who believe in that power, and use it, attain to a higher conception of matter as finally conquered by the spirit. If such a sanctification of matter were not already universally known, we should postulate its existence after our survey of the five other modes of apprehending the intimate reality of matter. If art supplements science, there must be something that is in a similar way supplemented by asceticism. This is generally called ritual, and consists chiefly in consciously creating, and skilfully applying, relics or sacraments to stimulate moral improvement in mankind.

The conscious production of relics in religious worship differs from active asceticism in much the same way as science differs from art. We have put science before art, though art is much older than science, because science has formulated the atomistic conception of matter, which is shown by the consideration of the four other methods to be thoroughly inadequate. Out of the immense wealth of human experience with respect to matter, atomism takes into account only the oldest science, namely astronomy. It is not a whirl of dust, nor the contemplation of the stars, nor the ravishing spectacle of fascinating *bayadères*, that will reveal to the thinker the deepest mystery of matter. We approach this goal through asceticism, and find its most subtle symbol in the Holy Grail, or in the Host exposed to the adoration of the faithful as the body of Christ.

The 'body of Christ' is a body in which there is no longer any rebellion against the omnipotence of the spirit, and which becomes therefore a source of spiritual power. Matter, created by the Fall of angels and of men, which produced stones and beasts, reaches at last a noble purpose when it is transubstantiated and its baleful influence is thus abolished.

This conception of sacramental transubstantiation, created by religious ritual, is the most original contribution towards the solution of the mystery of matter. The Church claims that bread and wine, serving as food and drink, can be so inwardly changed as to become the 'body of Christ'; that is, the immediate instrument through which Christ Himself acts on His worshippers. We call 'body' the immediate tool of the spirit, and it is easy to understand that if a close connection is created between any matter and a commanding spirit, we may say that such matter has become the 'body' of that spirit, or that the spirit has 'incarnated', taking that particular matter as its 'body'.

The claim of the Church is that it has the power to establish, through the rite of consecration, such a close immediate connection between a wafer or chalice of wine and the very spirit of Christ. There is nothing repugnant to reason in such a claim, though the proof is not easy, as it rests upon the proven sanctity of those who make use of this means of contact with their Lord.

But, for the metaphysician, the conception of the transubstantiation of matter has its value independently of the proof based upon moral consequences. This conception is the ultimate application of a faith in relics to the religious life, and leads to a still wider application of the same faith to social and political activity, culminating in national life. A relation similar to that between art and business exists at a higher level between religious worship and national life, so that national life, rightly understood, becomes the final test of our conception of relics and sacraments on a universal scale, embracing the whole of material existence.

CHAPTER VIII

National Life

Sacramental transubstantiation in religious ritual is concerned only with insignificant quantities of matter selected for that purpose. The generalisation of that process requires a closer relationship between those who are entrusted with the mission of carrying it out than has ever existed for any other purposes. It seems very difficult to conceive any closer union between men than the link which exists between perfect lovers forming a union for the purpose of giving birth to saints of genius.

This is a noble task, and the link between the parents of such offspring is a holy link. But it is limited to two individuals and based on sexual difference, which implies also a contrast in their activities. If men join together for a thorough transformation of material life, their numbers should not be limited, and their contact ought to embrace all possible activities, irrespective of sex, age, birth, profession, character and capacity.

Such a group of spirits united in a common mission on earth is called a nation, and national life is intimately associated with a providentially assigned national territory in which the national mission is destined to be fulfilled. Therefore national life has a material object—the adaptation of a certain territory to the accepted mission.

The relation of spirit to matter in national life differs from that observed in science, art, business, training and ritual; firstly, because it implies a social union of many individuals in a common task, and secondly, because in national life a whole territory becomes the object of human activity. Consequently, if the whole surface of the earth were divided into national territories and if each nation sincerely accepted its divine mission, the whole planet would undergo a transformation similar to sacramental transubstantiation.

All the other human activities which gave us experience of matter were limited to relatively small quantities of matter, acted upon by individuals. It is only national life that embraces the whole matter of a country, and if all countries were subjected to such national activity, the whole matter of the planet would soon be included.

Such activity must utilise all the preceding methods, and all the types of men we have seen engaged in various pursuits. The scientist has to show how his knowledge can be applied to the fulfilment of the national mission. The artist discovers that all his inspirations lead to an expression of the national spirit in works of art which manifest his nation's share in the universal life. The man of business, as soon as a national consciousness is awakened in him, ceases to consider his personal business individually, and looks at national business as a whole. Training leads to efficiency in such national business, and individual achievement becomes instrumental to the perfection of national life in general. Even religious ritual attains a national importance, as religion is a national asset, a means towards the fulfilment of the national mission.

The national territory is transformed in many ways by national life. But to understand this transformation we must extend our idea of what is supposed to happen when a material object becomes a relic of a saint or creative genius. Here the whole territory has to be so permeated by the national spirit as to become a lasting relic of the nation. This means that the spiritual influences of our ancestors have been somehow accumulated and fixated in the territory of our country, so that our contact with its soil becomes for us a source of inspiration, revealing to each his individual share in the work of the nation.

Such a material concentration of spiritual power requires an exceptional stability in the link uniting men with the soil, as well as permanence and continuity in their endeavours to conquer that soil thoroughly for spiritual purposes. National life in this way produces a relic having sacramental power.

The reality of this power can be ascertained only by those who are aware of the charm of their country, and who are conscious of their intimate connection with it. It begins as the love of a man's birthplace, but it grows until this love embraces the whole country in which his nation has to fulfil its mission.

As national life in this sense is of comparatively recent growth, we cannot expect many inhabitants in each country to have such consciousness of their intimate and permanent association with that country. But as soon as anybody has reached that stage, the consequence will be his decision to live for ever in that country, and the decay of his body at death will not hinder him from building in due time another body in which to continue his work. National tasks cannot be accomplished in a single life. Whoever becomes aware of such tasks has to live many lives in order to carry out his aspirations.

Thus national life becomes the common action of a group of spirits in a country given to them by Providence, in order to contribute their share towards an improvement in the life of mankind. A national mission has meaning only in relation to the universal life of humanity.

The goal is called *the Kingdom of God on earth.* It cannot be accomplished by a medley of peoples fighting with each other and envying each other, but only by true nations, which are the organs of humanity as the parts of a body are organs of that body. Nations having a common aim, the Kingdom of God,

83   6-2

are in natural harmony with each other, and not in that eternal state of war which has lasted for thousands of years between neighbouring countries.

National consciousness destroys tribal selfishness, and establishes such a link between the territory and its inhabitants that only their own territory suits them, and they do not envy their neighbours, nor wish to rob them of any part of their territory.

The frontiers of aggressive states are accidental results of wars and peace treaties. The frontiers of national territories depend on the special experiences that link each individual with his home and his nation. Such frontiers are the result of age-long activities, and are not always as easy to define as in the case of Italy or Spain or Great Britain.

The great majority of men have not yet acquired the national consciousness that unites each individual to his own country. It may take thousands of years before every inhabitant of Poland knows for certain whether he is a Pole, or not. But when this state is reached it will be found, naturally, that the country inhabited by true Poles is Poland, and no wars or treaties will be needed to fix its natural frontiers. It will become evident where the Polish spirit has carried out the work of creating that 'relic' called Poland through its national activities.

New laws will be formulated for the rectification of old frontiers, so that each nation acquires the territory that naturally belongs to it, without strife or envy. Meanwhile old state frontiers may remain, with increasing rights for national minorities living within these state frontiers, until all the inhabitants have settled according to their national consciousness, and have thus defined the frontiers of a national territory.

In a few cases these frontiers are determined by nature; for instance, the Pyrenees separate France from Spain. In other cases only national life and the will of the inhabitants of a territory will settle them gradually, when each citizen has decided in what country he wishes to live and to what nation he belongs. We have here to deal with a peculiar relation of man to matter which is hidden in each soul and admits of no objective proof, thus resembling sacramental transubstantiation.

But hidden things may nevertheless be real: this is the lesson of ritual, which finds its widest application in the mysterious link between a man and his country, a link continuously intensified by national life, until no doubt remains, at least for those who have actively participated in historical events of decisive importance. The heroic defence of Lwów, in November 1918, confirmed the Polish character of that city, just as the glorious days of the same month, when the Germans had to leave Poznań, showed Poznań to be truly Polish. Not only military events have such significance. The reality which we have to recognise is the link between a man and a place, and

85

also between a man and his nation. The belonging of places to nations results from the testimony of the individual inhabitants of each place. If a place is providentially destined for a certain nation, the number of inhabitants of that nation will increase in it, until a unanimous vote accomplishes the peaceful annexation of that place to the national territory.

We speak here of events which have as yet but rarely happened, as when the cities of Prussia and Pomerania in 1454 desired to be incorporated in the Polish republic, or when Nice and Savoy joined France in 1860, or when Venice joined Italy in 1866, or when the Ionian Islands joined Greece in 1864.

These are examples of what is likely to happen more often in the future through smaller units of territory joining a national state. Plebiscites are not essential in such cases; they only confirm a natural, existing relationship. Wilno was Polish for centuries before the vote of 1922 confirmed this to the world. When all such questions are decided, each nation will own its territory and improve that territory through all the means of science, art and business, while highly trained individuals will make it easier and easier for each succeeding generation to subdue material nature to spiritual forces, until each country becomes really one with its inhabitants, and material appearances are the outward expression of spiritual realities.

This process of a deeper penetration of matter by

86

national life is of such recent origin that very few living men can be thoroughly aware of it, and the unprecedented crime of three tyrannical dynasties which thrice partitioned Poland was needed to show the world an immortal example of a national life surviving the direst political persecution and the oppression of hostile governments established by force of arms in a free country.

The resurrection of Poland in 1918, a hundred and twenty-three years after its destruction by three powerful states, has shown for ever that material oppression cannot destroy a nation. National life acts independently of arbitrary violence, and offers a sublime example of the supremacy of spirit over matter. The influence of a nation over its predestined territory goes deeper, and is more thorough, than any other activity of the spirit, for it includes all other activities in a synthetic effort whose aim transcends all lesser human aims: the redemption of mankind from the result of the Fall and the realisation of the Kingdom of God on earth.

This process goes further than the activities of art, business or ritual. It must be integral, complete, absolute, signifying the decisive triumph of spirit over matter throughout the whole earth. If similar struggles are taking place elsewhere, the victory of the Spirit on earth will affect the whole of Heaven and acquire universal importance.

This victory reveals at the same time a new aspect

of matter, unknown to science, art, business, training and ritual. We learn that elementary gross matter, the soil under our feet, may become an object of love, and that love has the power of accumulating incredible spiritual forces even in such matter, without any process of selection, as in art, business, training and ritual. Here, for the first time the whole of matter becomes the object of a transformation brought about by spiritual love. The soil of our country exercises over us a power that is both magical and mystical. We look upon it as upon a 'relic' of heroic ancestors, and it inspires us to emulate them, and to strive to make our earth more like the sun—a shining abode of genius and sanctity, a true paradise of boundless happiness. The words of any human language are inadequate to express that reality which will be more and more fully revealed as men learn to love their work and the country for which they work. Nations will thus attain a higher standard of mutual co-operation, until the members of each nation act as one soul, and look upon the soil of their country, with all its beauties and all its wealth, as a well-trained body for the expression of the national spirit.

CHAPTER IX

Theory of Matter

We have now examined seven different methods by which the human spirit comes into immediate contact with matter and gathers experience of the material world. Let us carefully consider that classification which has never as yet been attempted by philosophers or psychologists.

A very simple experiment may enable every reader to test the objective value of our survey. Let him explain to anybody the difference between science and art in virtue of the special experiences gained by the scientist and artist respectively, according to Chapters III and IV. Then let him ask in what ways other than those of art and science men come into contact with and experience matter. He will find that very few will hit upon asceticism, or training or sexual life, as a means of becoming acquainted with the matter of our body—and fewer still will be aware of ritual as a human activity in which spirit confronts matter. But if these aspects of the relation between spirit and matter are explained, it will not be difficult to show that training, sex and ritual, reveal something of matter that neither science nor art could make clear. It may be more difficult to obtain the recognition of business activity as an independent way towards the knowledge and mastery of matter, while our classification of business men may not convince everybody. But the greatest difficulty will be to demonstrate that the patriot's love of his country opens a new view of the relation between matter and spirit.

Such experiments will show that it is nearly impossible to find anybody who could answer our question by detailing the seven ways we have defined, though almost everybody, if he is told about them, will admit and understand their reality, and nobody will be able to suggest other methods than those we have mentioned.

Therefore our classification is of importance, as it permits a real survey of what we can know about matter. Such a classification corresponds to an existing reality; it teaches us something about ourselves and also about matter. We have to admit that there are only the seven following methods of gathering experience of matter.

1. *Science* reduces matter to 'bodies in movement'. But even the smallest bodies have a size and shape and are therefore not matter, but a product of matter, so that we have to seek some other way in order to reach matter in its immediate contact with spirit.

2. *Art* shapes matter and extends the notion of matter from visible bodies to invisible sounds and

words, which are the matter of music and poetry. The matter of art has forms more various than the matter of science, and is further removed from the overwhelming fixity and rigidity of astronomical and geological matter.

3. *Business* acts on a vaster scale than art and leads us towards the domination of the whole matter of the earth. It starts with hunting and fishing, rises to pastoral and agricultural activity, produces industry, commerce, banking, economic, social and political organisation. Physicians, lawyers, clergymen and soldiers are subsidiary to production in so far as they prevent losses and help thereby towards the human mastery of the material world.

4. *Training* has to do with the matter of our own body. It starts with the negative discipline of asceticism and rises to the positive ideal of a strong, healthy and beautiful body thoroughly dominated by the spirit.

5. *Sexual life* concerns the experience gathered through the intimate relations of two bodies and souls of different sex. The highest stage is the voluntary procreation of healthy and beautiful organisms, controlled by souls in which sanctity is allied to genius.

6. *Ritual* is concerned with relics and sacraments. It brings about the transubstantiation of matter for the moral improvement of human life.

7. *National life* brings about a similar transubstantiation on a much vaster scale, with the ultimate

aim of sanctifying the whole earth when divided into a few national territories cultivated and improved by true nations.

These seven methods are generally known, but their importance appears in full only if we look at them as supplementing one another in the immense process of sanctification and spiritualisation of matter which is taking place throughout the whole universe. Then we become aware of what the seven methods have in common and how, when taken together, they lead us to a discovery of the very nature of matter.

Matter then appears as that which is opposed to spirit, offering a passive resistance to the activity of spirit. We see how spirit overcomes this resistance, and finally subjugates the whole of material existence to spiritual power. We cannot define matter in terms of something else, as for instance 'bodies in movement'. Matter is a kind of reality which we perceive more immediately in our own body than in any bodies moving around us. In this immediate awareness of our body there is no particular image of movements, but rather a hindrance to every movement intended by the spirit.

The movements of our body as opposed to the passivity of matter are produced by our will. Matter has no existence save in relation to mind. It is *that which resists our will*, until it becomes a relic, a sacrament, or the national territory of a truly living nation.

There are two fundamental experiences of the

spirit in relation to matter. We either passively perceive matter, or actively shape and transform it. Perception and action supplement each other, so that we perceive an actual state, and produce another state in conformity with the needs of our spirit. Materialisation stands above perception, and therefore a temptation overcome, or a consecrated sacrament, affords us a better explanation of the nature of matter than any conception of 'bodies in movement'.

Though the majority of mankind may ignore relics and sacraments and the mystical link between a nation and its country, it is only in religious ritual and national life that we find the ultimate solution of the problem of matter. Matter ceases to be a temptation, a hindrance, a limitation of the spirit, and becomes its obedient tool, giving objective permanence to the spirit's creations.

Whether matter resists or obeys our will, that awareness of resistance or mastery furnishes us with the chief means of comprehending the essence of matter. It is nothing by itself, and becomes real only in conflict with spirit. We call 'matter' that which either serves us or hinders our activity. Any bodily shape is a modification of matter, a determination of its being. Matter as such, apart from spirit, has no form, no limits, no quality. It cannot be identified with space, though we conceive it as existing in space. When we say that matter fills space, we mean that space limits matter. Space and matter correspond to one another as different aspects of a reality that is opposed to the spiritual reality of our self. Such conceptions cannot be defined by each other, or explained by something else. Space, matter, cause, and aim are ideas created by the spirit to designate what is not spirit.

The reality which makes the impression of matter on spirit might be the activity of inferior spirits mastered by temptation. In a similar way we ourselves become material through yielding to temptation. The whole material world is that which resists the activity of spirit until it is finally controlled by spirit. Thus, matter is relative, growing or decaying according to the increasing or decreasing power of the spirit. The spirit creates or destroys matter, and the indestructibility of matter is an illusion of those who identify matter with spirit as the only reality.

The seven ways of gaining experience of matter clearly show the insufficiency of materialism, and the inadequacy of any conception of a permanent and indestructible material world. This material world undergoes continuous changes, not only of quality but also of quantity. Every act of free-will may increase or decrease the materiality of our own body, and we are constantly creating, transforming or annihilating matter by our free decisions.

It is only if we imagine matter as a conglomeration of bodies of determinate size moving with measurable velocity that it may appear to us as indestructible.

As soon as we extend our experience of matter to such subtler realities as unuttered words, or victorious temptations, we must recognise the power of the spirit to create or destroy matter, and then the matter of stones and stars ceases to be the chief example of material reality.

We are enabled to appreciate the gross matter of bodies by recognising its fundamental similarity to the much subtler matter undergoing transubstantiation. In both cases it is something manifesting a decreasing resistance to spirit. The capacity of the spirit to overcome that resistance and to attain mastery defines matter. While spirit has a real and absolute existence, the existence of matter is relative, depends on spirit, and might be conceived as a changing state of inferior spirits, gradually to be abolished.

Such a conception of matter will not prevent us from applying number and measure to material appearances such as are known to us at definite stages of our spiritual existence. We may number molecules and evaluate the mass of atoms or the size of electrons, without forgetting that they are only convenient fictions of our own minds.

We know such convenient fictions even in the spiritual world. Our mind has a peculiar power of creating them. If we distinguish, in the same individual, the artist from the husband or father, if we imagine as does Benda in his *Ordination*, a struggle

95

going on between two different persons within the same living man, we know very well that no such real persons can have a separate and independent existence. They are merely convenient fictions for the purpose of describing the reality of the inner life of one and the same soul.

Those for whom the sight of a body in movement is more real than the struggle within the soul against an overwhelming temptation will try to explain temptation by the movement of atoms. But in the general scheme of existence the recognition of the reality of spiritual struggles corresponds to a higher stage than the perception or imagination of moving bodies. At each stage our awareness of matter varies, and tends either towards dematerialisation and sanctification of what remains material, or towards the degradation of what is spiritual. Matter in all its changing forms is the natural field for the exercise of spiritual powers. It is the enemy or adversary of the spirit, but may become its docile instrument.

Our true existence is spiritual, and as soon as we become aware of it we recognise matter as that which is not ourselves. Every definition explains what is unknown by what is known. Therefore, for a spirit the definition of matter as *negation of spirit* is very much more legitimate than the attempt to explain spirit as a movement of matter. Negation is intellectual, movement is material. We know thought as an activity of spirit, not of matter. Therefore our thought is led to an interpretation of matter in terms of spirit, and not in a contrary manner.

This is made evident if we survey and compare the different possible attitudes of spirit towards matter, and therefore a classification of these attitudes is a real problem of metaphysics and deserves the attention which has never yet been given to it.

Suppose we call up, in a long procession, the various types of mankind who deal with matter—astronomer, physicist, chemist, biologist, metapsychist, sculptor, architect, dancer, painter, musician, poet, actor, hunter, fisherman, herdsman, agriculturalist, engineer, merchant, banker, physician, lawyer, clergyman, soldier, statesman, ascetic, athlete, lover, priest, patriot—and ask them all: *What is matter?* Would most of them not agree in saying: 'it is what hinders us and what we wish to master'?

Thus the mere attempt to distinguish and classify the different ways in which man may deal with matter implies a theory of matter totally opposed to traditional atomism. Atomism strives to explain spiritual reality by the movements of bodies, while we have seen that bodies are materialisations produced by spirit. Science and worship are passive, or perceptive; while art, business, training and patriotism are active, or materialising. Sex is simultaneously active materialisation and passive perception. Perception as well as materialisation reveals matter as the negation of spirit, spirit as that which masters matter.

CHAPTER X

Idealism

As soon as materialism was formulated in the atomic theory of Democritus, a reaction against this theasy was inevitable. The attempt to explain all reality by movements of bodies was intolerable to those who were able to distinguish thought from sensations. Sensations are supposed to depend on some external reality, whereas thought is within our mind and obeys a logical necessity which differs from the mechanical necessity of physical movements.

Every thinker who thinks his own thoughts soon discovers the stupendous fact that his concepts may also be thought by others, and this identity of concepts in different minds is an identity such as we never find in material things. There are no two equal blades of grass or grains of sand, but the concept of equality was exactly the same in the mind of the ancient mathematician Euclid as it is in the mind of any schoolboy of our times.

This great discovery of the identity of concepts, formulated for the first time in the history of human thought by Plato, in the speech of Diotima in the *Banquet*, led him to the supposition that a concept might have its own existence, independently of any individual who entertained that concept. Such an objective reality has been called an *idea*. An idea is the supposed objective reality which we know subjectively as a concept, just as matter is the supposed objective reality corresponding to our subjective sensations.

The man of ideas belongs to an altogether different type from the man of sensations. It commonly happens that if the former gets enthusiastic over his ideas, he proceeds to a false generalisation similar to that of the materialist, and seeks to explain everything by eternal ideas, imagining that nothing else really exists.

We call such a man an *idealist*, and his conception of existence *idealism*. The term *idealism* has been constantly misused as denoting every possible theasy that contradicts materialism, because idealism was the oldest reaction to materialism. The faulty generalisation which extended the meaning of the term *idealism* to other theasies opposed to materialism must be set aside, if we desire a perfectly clear classification of theasies which have occurred in history, or which may possibly occur.

Idealism means the recognition of ideas as the only reality. Therefore Berkeley, who recognised the existence of God and of the soul, has wrongly been called an idealist. Plato was an idealist when he wrote the *Banquet*, the *Phaedo* and the *Republic*, but in the *Phaedrus* he discovered that ideas exist only in souls, and this truth was developed in the *Theae-tetus*, the *Parmenides*, the *Sophistes*, the *Politicus* and the *Philebus*.

Thus in Plato's later years idealism was abandoned; but as the later dialogues were less read than those in which the discovery of idealism had been enthusiastically proclaimed, Plato was held by most of his readers, throughout twenty-three centuries, to be merely an idealist.

This has greatly contributed to the confusion which led to the use of the term *idealism* to denote any philosophy which was not materialistic. Idealism and materialism were so much in view as the chief opposed ways of thinking that few people guessed the existence of other theasies, and most thinkers were classified as materialists or idealists, the term *idealist* being used as equivalent to anti-materialist or non-materialist.

The idealist seeks perfect consistency in his system of ideas, but he can attain it only by disregarding all ideas that are inconsistent with his main system. Every consistent idealistic system is built on a cemetery of rejected ideas. Idealism is logically the second stage, after materialism, in the quest for reality, because ideas form the chief content of consciousness after sensations, and because man usually becomes aware of his ideas later than of his sensations.

Ideas have a kind of reality within ourselves similar to the reality of matter, but different from the reality of the Self which includes and reconciles ideas and sensations. A sensation worked upon by thought becomes a perception, and perceptions are intermediate between sensations and ideas.

Materialism acknowledges as the only reality the objects of perceptions, while idealism insists on the reality of ideas, and looks even upon perceptions as ideas.

Idealists and materialists have argued for centuries without ever convincing one another. The opposition between materialism and idealism is based on the psychological difference between men of sensations and men of ideas. Though everybody has both sensations and ideas, there may be a predominance of sensations which leads to materialism, or a predominance of ideas which leads to idealism. Materialism and idealism are the two most obvious solutions of the riddle of existence, and the immense majority of living men are, even in our times, either materialists or idealists.

But in our quest for truth neither materialism nor idealism can satisfy us, because both are false generalisations. It is not true that everything is matter, for we have seen that a complete investigation of matter by all the methods accessible to man leads beyond matter to the existence of spirit. It is equally wrong to say that ideas are the only reality, as no idea has any real existence outside a thinking being, that is, a spirit.

Moreover, although a well-defined idea may be imparted to others and does not change, there is in individual minds a constant production of new ideas. This has the appearance of an evolution or growth of ideas, but really there is no growth of the same ideas, but a succession of similar ideas replacing one another.

This process is more intimately known to us than the movement of bodies in space, but if we follow up the analogy we might reach the conclusion that what appears to be the movement of the same body in space is nothing else than the materialisation and dematerialisation of many bodies succeeding one another. This again would prove that neither bodies nor ideas have any substantial existence, and that ideas are only products and instruments of the human spirit, even as matter has been shown to be a product and instrument of the spirit.

Idealism and materialism have much more in common than either materialists or idealists have ever recognised. These two first metaphysical alternatives constitute a logical dilemma, so that each horn points to the same conclusion. Both are intellectual reactions of human pride against the original religious revelation which taught of the soul, of the freedom of will, and of God, the Creator of the Universe.

This revelation was the experience of a few privileged sages, who asked the masses to believe them blindly, as not everybody was capable of experiencing a personal religious experience. Early thinkers rebelled, as subsequently did all those who had the ambition to find truth for themselves instead of accepting it blindly from some outstanding authority; these all sought their own way of explaining life and the world.

Just as Thales, living in a seaport and receiving more impressions from the sea than from anything else, came to the conclusion that water was everything and that nothing existed except water, so the men who were overflowing with sensations, overwhelmed by the impressions of the material world, declared that everything was matter, and became materialists. Others of a more refined mind, who did not care for sensations, but were enraptured by the beauty of ideas, declared that ideas were everything, and they became idealists.

Thus materialism and idealism are merely false generalisations based on personal experience, and they both agree in the rejection of religious authority and religious dogma. If everything is matter, then there is no soul, or what is called soul is nothing but a material appearance, neither free nor immortal. There is then nothing in the world except 'bodies in movement', obeying mechanical necessity, and in such a thoroughly material world there is no room for the soul. Some physicians boast that they have never found a soul while dissecting the brain. They tacitly assume that a soul should have a visible form like a body, because they are unable to imagine invisible and impalpable existence. For them there is no soul; the whole of reality is material and exists without beginning or end. There is also no room for God in such a universe. God and His creation become a futile invention of priests who cheat the people by pretending to know more than the average man.

Exactly the same conclusions are arrived at by consistent idealism, if we limit the meaning of this term to the philosophy which considers only ideas to be true substances. If ideas are everything, then the soul is a general idea, and the individual separate soul becomes a temporary illusion. Then also God is nothing but an eternal idea, not a real Being. The real world being a world of unchangeable ideas, it has never been created, and it is not guided by a wise Providence, because everything is settled for ever by the logical necessity which binds the ideas co-existing simultaneously in a single mind into a consistent system.

Individual freedom of will, just as much as individual life, is then an illusion. Nothing really happens; everything is for ever. Thus materialists and idealists, emancipated from blind belief in religious authority, came to the denial of the fundamental dogmas of every religion—a free immortal soul and an omnipotent, wise and just Creator. These first steps of the proud independent reason of man, unguided by God, led nowhere, and made seekers after truth appear to themselves as machines or impersonal ideas—that is, mere fancies.

The identity of the negative conclusions of both materialism and idealism remained unnoticed as long as the chief stress was laid on the difference between the two opposite metaphysical alternatives, according to which either everything was supposed to be matter or everything had to be conceived as thought. Idealism has almost as long a tradition historically as materialism, and every wave of materialism had its reaction in a wave of idealism. The primitive materialism of the Ionian philosophers was answered by the idealism of Pythagoras, contained in the prominence given by him to numbers. This, the oldest attempt at an explanation of reality through ideas, was not consistent, as the Pythagoreans also taught the existence of God and of the soul.

A more consistent idealism was introduced by Plato to counteract the materialism of Democritus, and since the modification of Platonic idealism by Aristotle this form of idealism remained essentially the same until a new attempt to formulate the idealistic theasy was made by Hegel. Hegelian idealism prevailed in the first half of the nineteenth century, and with slight transformations persists in the present day in such writers as F. H. Bradley (1846–1924), B. Bosanquet (1848–1923), B. Croce (b. 1866), G. Gentile (b. 1875).

But it is not in the form of systematic philosophy

taught by professional philosophers that idealism exercises the greatest influence. The idealist is very common among ordinary humanity, and he has many familiar names. He may be the doctrinaire who simplifies his conception of reality by adopting a narrow set of ideas, and who accepts no correction from experience; or he may be the fanatic sectarian in religion or politics who tests every truth by its conformity with a simple formula accepted as infallible (such as, for instance, the cause of every evil is: the Jews—or the Jesuits—or the Freemasons—or alcohol—or tobacco—or democracy—or universal suffrage—or war—or wealth—or anything else). Or he may be the inquisitor who would like to burn all who do not agree with him, because he considers his own ideas to be absolute truth established for ever.

Such types of men judge the whole of reality according to ideas contained in their individual consciousness, preconceived notions, or prejudices of all kinds. Whenever we see the thought of anybody identified with absolute reality, in disregard of actual experience, we have to deal with idealism. Idealism has not, like materialism, been silenced for seventeen centuries; it has been taught without intermission ever since Plato and Aristotle. It has penetrated human consciousness to a greater extent than any other theasy. Most of those who would scorn to be materialists are now idealists of some kind. And even the materialists, in so far as they accept scientific

atomism, have become idealists. Whenever we meet
what is called a *system*, it is easy to discover that it is
a product of idealism.

Intellectual formulas exceeding our experience and
purporting to explain all reality belong to idealism.
And strangely enough, the idealist—who judges of
all reality according to his personal thought, who
identifies the universe with himself, and credits it
with his own understanding—does not remark that
he is himself a true being, distinct and different from
all other beings.

His own individuality is neglected like all other
individualities, and only general abstractions or ideas
exist for him. For the sake of an idea he is capable
of killing or torturing others, and even himself.
Idealism has justified the utmost cruelty, and every
kind of persecution, in public and private relations.
When the materialist Lucretius in his poem *De
Rerum Natura* exclaims 'tantum religio potuit suadere
malorum!' (lib. I, verse 101) in speaking of the sacrifice
of Iphigenia for the success of the Greek fleet, he does
not mean true religion, but idealism in religion, the
rigidity of an intellectual formula in disregard of
human feelings.

We often decide our most important actions according to such formulas, presuming their general
and universal validity. We say approvingly that
somebody is a 'man of principle'. Such a man is an
idealist who subordinates his conscience to a set of

principles. The rule of ideas over the world is a result of the peculiar power of thought. We feel a need to explain everything by thought, to establish fixed rules for our conduct, and these rules are intellectual formulas which may disregard legitimate emotions, like pity and parental love, as in the case of Iphigenia.

All kinds of religious and political fanaticism, party strife and tyranny, result from idealism. Thought easily becomes despotic, when those who are strong feel unable to convince their opponents by logical arguments. There are other elements in consciousness besides ideas, and life is essentially irrational. Reality cannot be completely embraced by thought, nor can conduct always be defined by principles. This is the weakness of idealism, which leads to another theasy, following after materialism and idealism, and coming next to them in the numbers of its followers. It is an attempt at a conciliation of extremes, a first synthesis of opposite views in a higher unity, represented by a third type of thinker, who differs from both the materialist and the idealist.

CHAPTER XI

Pantheism

In addition to sensations and ideas we find in our consciousness emotions or feelings, and there are men in whom neither sensations nor ideas are as dominant as feelings. They suffer when they witness the cruelty of idealists or the roughness of materialists. They long for the harmony and unity of the whole. This type of man created the third great conception of existence, usually called *pantheism*.

Real existence for the pantheist is neither material nor ideal, but essential oneness; and this Unity of Being has two parallel aspects which are, respectively, the material and the intellectual aspects of existence. Extension and thought become attributes of Being, and in the search for a term to convey his enthusiasm, the pantheist has dared to commit the sacrilege of using for that impersonal Unity of Being the most exalted name of religious tradition, the name of God.

He professes to think that everything is God, and therefore he is called a *pantheist*. But the pantheist is always an atheist, and he accepts the whole inheritance of idealism and materialism in the denial of an individual free soul and an omnipotent, wise and just Creator.

Pantheism is the conception of the man of emotion, with an exalted consciousness of the Unity of Being and the identity of matter and thought. The birthplace of pantheism was the Greek colony of Elea in Southern Italy, where Xenophanes (580–480 B.C.) taught Parmenides (540–470 B.C.) and Parmenides had as his disciple Zeno of Elea.

This old tradition of Elea was renewed and perfected by Spinoza (A.D. 1632–1677) in modern times. He gave the title *Ethica* to his chief work, though pantheism implies such a rigorous determinism that no room is left for moral responsibility, and therefore no rules of conduct can have any meaning or influence. The best known living representative of pantheism in the English-speaking world is Samuel Alexander, who delivered the Gifford Lectures in 1916–1918, afterwards published in two large volumes in 1920 under the title *Space, Time and Deity*.

That a pantheist may preach his atheism in a course of Gifford Lectures, and invoke an abstract Deity, the contrary of a living personal God, in the title of his chief work, shows that the old Eleatic doctrine remains alive and active. The conclusion of Alexander's work (vol. II, p. 429) deserves to be mentioned here as the latest *credo* of contemporary pantheism. He says: 'In the hierarchy of qualities the next higher quality to the highest attained is deity. God is the whole universe engaged in process towards the emergence of this new quality, and religion is the sentiment in us that we are drawn towards him, and caught in the movement of the world to a higher level of existence'.

Although Alexander claims that his conception is rather theistic than pantheistic, and that in different respects it belongs to theism as well as to pantheism (vol. II, p. 394), we cannot doubt, according to the above conclusion which identifies God with the universe, that it is pantheistic and therefore atheistic.

But the importance of pantheism in modern life is not limited to systematic expositions of pantheistic philosophy by professional philosophers. Many men of all professions are pantheists without being aware of it, and pantheism is manifest in religious indifference, which excludes prayer and creates the illusion that there is no reality beyond human life.

The consistent pantheist is not a cruel inquisitor, such as the idealist has sometimes been. He is extremely tolerant, as he fancies that nothing really matters, nobody is really responsible, and everything that happens is inevitable. International pacifism, which is sometimes inclined to overrule international justice, is one of the many manifestations of this pantheistic attitude. The American New Thought movement is also a pantheistic growth. When men cease to look up to their Creator, they divinify themselves and think themselves omnipotent. Faith in unlimited progress, regardless of human efforts, belongs to this pantheistic theasy.

An impersonal power is supposed to act through all human individuals, but no individual has a real immortal existence. Individuals are only modes or appearances of one universal reality. Such religious conceptions as duty, responsibility, sin, remorse, fear of eternal damnation, hope of eternal salvation, become meaningless if there is no difference between creature and Creator, and if each of us is only a passing appearance of one universal 'becoming'.

Pantheism is superior to materialism and idealism, in being more consistent than either. It embraces intellectual and material reality on equal terms, without allowing the predominance of one-sided thought or of sensual enjoyment. Pantheists are unobtrusive, peaceful men, not likely to fight for their convictions, and ready to agree to everything and to reconcile all contradictions.

But although they are convinced that the world progresses by itself, they feel unable to contribute anything of their own towards the result. By repeating to themselves that they are nothing, that nothing matters, that only an anonymous Whole works through them, they have sunk into real nothingness, and have lost the courage of any original initiative.

Pantheism, by denying that anything really new can happen, by cutting man off from the personal source of every lofty inspiration, prevents creative activity, and makes this world a very dull place to live in. It is, however, a step beyond materialism and idealism, though it rarely avoids oscillating between materialistic and idealistic tendencies, and most pantheists incline to a materialist attitude, especially if they put Space-Time above Deity.

These first three steps in the quest for truth—materialism, idealism and pantheism—were made by the Greeks more than two thousand years ago, and we may class them all together under the name of *monism*. Monism is an essentially irreligious conception of life: it is the intellectual reaction of all those who have not yet reached personal religious experience, and who disdain to accept blindly the revelation of others.

Such men seek reality first in matter, then in ideas, finally in the unity of the Whole; but in all these attempts to understand and explain reality they completely ignore themselves and their own individual existence. As long as either sensations or thoughts or emotions prevail in the soul, the individual Self is not manifest, because each of these experiences is common to many. If I see or hear something, I expect others to see or hear exactly the same thing. Similarly with our thoughts or emotions. They are impersonal; instead of saying: 'I see', 'I think', 'I feel', we might say: 'it is seen, thought, felt'. The object—sensations, thoughts and emotions—overwhelms and benumbs the subject, i.e. the soul or spirit.

This is the negative conclusion of the first metaphysical dilemma: whether the world is material or ideal, I am nearly nothing in relation to the universe of matter or of ideas. And pantheism confirms this nothingness of the Self.

The long development of monism—in its three stages of materialism, idealism and pantheism—reached, however, one positive and very important conclusion. In opposition to all appearances there is something that is True Being, and this is indestructible. For the materialist this True Being was *Matter*; for the idealist, *Ideas*; for the pantheist, *the Universe*. But they all agreed that true permanent indestructible Being exists. This has become an indubitable dogma of every later philosophy. If anything other than matter, ideas, the universe, should be discovered to be True Being, it also will have a legitimate claim to be eternal and indestructible.

This is a result which remains as the foundation of metaphysics. The quest for truth has become, through two thousand years of monistic endeavours, a metaphysical pursuit—the formulation of the fundamental metaphysical problem, consisting in the answer to the questions: What really exists? What is the difference between appearance and reality?

We have seen how the false appearance created by scientific atomism was destroyed by the impartial study of all the seven ways leading to the knowledge of matter. Behind the appearance of matter we have in all seven methods discovered the reality of the spirit. We may now ask whether the appearance created by the world of ideas can be similarly destroyed by a comparative study of several ways leading to the knowledge of ideas.

One of these ways is obviously science, as it was for matter. Science defines and classifies ideas, utilising them for the knowledge of truth. Is there any other way leading to the same goal? It is easy to see that art is not limited to shaping matter, but that in the process of artistic materialisation ideas are intuitively perceived and the necessary form created for their expression.

Intuition differs from reasoning and attains its aim more immediately. But while science can deal with ideas as eternally existing without change, intuition creates new ideas, and rejects those which have become useless. We may disregard the thinker in reasoning, because it is supposed to be always the same for all thinking beings, but if a new idea is suddenly perceived by our intuition, we soon convince ourselves that it does not exist equally for all, but depends on the quality of the seer. This emancipates us from the fixity and rigidity of the ideas known to science.

Beyond intuition there is a third way of reaching ideas, called inspiration or revelation, in which we become aware, not only of the spirit receiving the gift, but also of the infinitely superior Giver. This experience transcends the limits of monism and leads us up to a higher theasy, which, in contrast to monism, may be called pluralism, as it implies a plurality of spirits, each individually different from all others.

We have then to abandon the indestructibility of matter and the immutability of ideas, finding true beings which are neither matter, nor ideas, but which create matter and ideas. This is, in general, the end of pantheism and of monism, which, in view of the higher inspiration, must be recognised as inadequate for the understanding of True Being.

CHAPTER XII

Spiritualism

Apart from sensations, ideas and emotions, there is in human consciousness another element which is usually obscured by the tumult these arouse, but which in some men attains mastery and distinguishes them from the rest of humanity. Men of this fourth type are those for whom *will* predominates over all other contents of consciousness and controls them. The will is the first individualising factor in consciousness, because the will of each man is not only not necessarily the same as the wills of other men, but is often in conflict with their wills.

The men of will are not on an equality. There is a training which increases will power, and an inborn capacity resulting from pre-existence. The law of will-training is that every efficient effort increases will power and every failure weakens it.

Successful efforts depend on the prudent choice of immediate aims, in relation to circumstances. The man of will, after many successful efforts, arrives naturally at a peculiar experience, which is the discovery of Self, giving absolute certainty to the individual that he really exists, that he is himself a 'true being', and therefore eternal and indestructible.

On this true existence of the spirit is built the fourth great conception of existence, which is called *spiritualism*—or the philosophy of the spirit—or sometimes *personalism*. Unfortunately, it has often been misnamed idealism, because the age-long opposition between materialism and idealism led to calling every philosophy 'idealism' which was opposed to materialism: for example, the philosophy of Berkeley or of Boström. These philosophers were not idealists, but spiritualists, in the sense in which we are now using these terms.

The term *spiritualism* has been corrupted in England and America by being applied to something totally different from spiritualism, namely *spiritism*, or the invocation of the souls of the dead. Spiritism, like spiritualism, was born in France and came from France to England. Though spiritualism is much older, spiritism is more popular, and spiritists like to miscall themselves spiritualists.

We cannot, however, give up a useful term of international significance because it has been illegitimately appropriated by a modern sect in an exceptionally unphilosophic country. We shall therefore maintain the name of spiritualism for that conception of existence which is based on the discovery of the individual spirit, and is characteristic of the men of will, as distinguished from the men of sensations, ideas, or emotions.

Spiritualism really preceded monism in religious

teaching, being the conception of all those who had a personal experience of God. We also find spiritualism in the later works of Plato, written after he had given up his early idealism.[1] But this spiritualism remained unnoticed, until the great French thinker Descartes gave it a new start in the seventeenth century, and was followed by his great disciple Malebranche. Since then spiritualism has become the French national philosophy.

At the beginning of the nineteenth century it was represented by the great metaphysician, Maine de Biran, and, through the influence of Victor Cousin, was introduced into the teaching of all French universities. A great succession of original thinkers— such as Gratry, Vacherot, Ravaisson, Secretan, Naville, Janet, Caro, Lachelier, Boutroux and others —have worked out various problems of spiritualism, and at the beginning of the twentieth century Renouvier undertook to give a synthetic exposition of this view of life.

Spiritualism provides a philosophic foundation for the religious dogmas rejected by monism. However, a conflict arises at a higher level between pantheism and spiritualism, similar to the old quarrel between materialists and idealists. Pantheism, in its materialistic as well as in its idealistic form, is the outcome

[1] See the author's work *Plato's Logic* (Longmans, 1897), in which this aspect of later Platonism is clearly determined, with full philological justification of the difference between earlier and later works of Plato.

of Greek philosophy, and in modern times has been prevalent in Germany, while spiritualism has become the national philosophy of the French. The political conflicts between the two neighbours are due to a great extent to a difference in their fundamental attitude towards reality, which is manifest, on the one hand, in German monism, and, on the other, in French spiritualism.

Spiritualism, though born in France, is a conception of Life and Being for all nations, and is the inevitable fourth stage in the quest for truth. In the development of the individual, materialism corresponds to the attitude of the child, idealism is the natural outlook of the young man who begins to think, and pantheism follows, when feelings and emotions rise to the highest intensity. In riper years the struggle against obstacles and the fulfilment of self-imposed tasks lead those who have experienced the discovery of the Self to spiritualism.

The simultaneous existence of materialists, idealists and pantheists is sufficiently accounted for by the innate inequality of men, which is the result of pre-existence; that is, of long-past, forgotten achievements or failures of each individual soul. In the general history of mankind spiritualism is so recent that it has not yet prevailed over the older views. Outside France, the national philosophy of Sweden, personified in Boström, may claim to be called spiritualism. In England, among the writers of the last generation, James Ward must be considered as a spiritualist. Idealism and pantheism have eminent followers in England, and even materialism is not quite extinct. Idealism and materialism usually disdain their primitive forms, and are merged into some kind of pantheism by the use of such negative terms as the 'unknowable' (Herbert Spencer), or the 'unconscious' (von Hartmann, Freud).

Thus pantheism and spiritualism are the conflicting powers in modern times, as were materialism and idealism in antiquity. A conciliation of these extremes is possible only if it can be shown that both may lead to the same conclusion, even as idealism and materialism led to pantheism. Such a synthesis is very much more difficult at a higher stage, for the opposition between the men of emotions (pantheists) and the men of will (spiritualists) goes much deeper than the opposition between the men of sensations and the men of thought. We cannot exclude thought from the life of reasonable beings, but we may reduce individual will to insignificance. Materialists could never avoid some thinking, but pantheists do not need to will anything in particular. And the difficulty is increased by the apparent moral superiority of the pantheist, who, if he is consistent, eliminates selfishness and egotism from his life, while the man of will has his own aims and cannot ignore himself.

This contrast has been exemplified in two great

religions of mankind. Buddhism teaches renuncia-
tion, the extinction of individual will. Christianity
is essentially spiritualistic, and the full growth of
spiritualism was possible only in such a thoroughly
Christian country as France, which has been called
'the eldest daughter of the Church'. Many simple
believers who know nothing of philosophy and are
not interested in philosophical discussions are
spiritualists because they are Christians.

This means that they have a strong consciousness
of liberty and responsibility and know themselves
as immortal beings. The discovery of one's own
existence leads to the admission of a similar immortal existence of others, and this implies a world
of souls not equal to one another, but forming an
ascending scale with a summit—the Highest Being.

Logically the spiritualist admits a Highest Being,
but this does not yet imply creation. Consistent
spiritualism in its first stages is rather inclined to
consider souls as the materialist considers atoms,
having neither beginning nor end. We are naturally
inclined to think that what has a beginning must have
an end, and in the first fervour of the discovery of
our immortality we admit eternal pre-existence as a
matter of course.

This point is of great importance in our classification, because usually most spiritualists have gone
farther and admitted a Creator. This was due to the
influence of Christianity as a religion, and not to the

logical implications of the discovery of Self, which is the foundation of spiritualism. This discovery that 'I am a true Being, an immortal soul', seems rather to imply logically that 'I have always existed', for the same reasons which make the materialist credit atoms with eternal existence.

Spiritualists who admit that they are creatures transcend pure and consistent spiritualism; they accept a religious dogma having another origin. There is a serious logical difficulty in this admission, which really belongs to a higher theasy. According to the common tradition of materialism, idealism and pantheism, True Being was indestructible, but also uncreated. If therefore we wish to apply the old dogma of all monistic philosophy to the newly discovered reality of souls, we shall have to pay for their immortality the heavy price of their eternal pre-existence, in opposition to the Christian dogma which teaches us that we are creatures of a Creator.

The only way out of this difficulty for spiritualists, if they wish to accept the religious dogma of creation, will be to say that we were created *out of time* or *in eternity*. But this is by no means easy to understand, as religious tradition usually presupposes creation in time, a definite number of years ago.

In order to justify eternal creation we have to prove the so-called ideality of time, which means that time exists only in human thought. This is no theological heresy, and has been admitted by many theologians, though it goes very much against the common-sense of the average Christian.

We need not discuss this problem here, as we do not intend to remain at the level of pure and consistent spiritualism. What really imports for the ulterior development of our argument is that this pure consistent spiritualism, based on the activity of will and the discovery of an immaterial and immortal Self, knows God only as the Highest Being, but not yet as the Creator of the universe; and it is such a spiritualism that is in conflict with contemporary pantheism.

Besides Christianity, it is chiefly the world of business in its higher stages that leads to spiritualism. Hunters, fishermen, herdsmen, agriculturalists, may be materialists or men of sensations. But industry, commerce, politics, and the professional activities of the lawyer, the physician, the clergyman, the soldier, are a constant exercise of the power of will over matter, and if the will attains its aims, the individual learns to distinguish himself from others, to feel himself a power and a true being.

He may be held back from this awakening because his thought is concentrated on material tasks and rarely rises above these immediate aims, but the most successful business men are likely to reach a spiritualistic attitude, even if they do not care for the philosophic theasy. Positive training also is chiefly a discipline of will, and, as such, a source of the consciousness of Self which is the foundation of spiritualism. But spiritualism as a theasy above pantheism, and independent of religious revelation, is not frequent among practical people of any kind, as they usually lack the necessary leisure and the intellectual eagerness to cause them to travel very far beyond tradition. They generally accept a denominational creed if they are religious, or pantheism if they are irreligious.

CHAPTER XIII

Mysticism

The solution of the conflict between pantheism and spiritualism can be supplied only by a new element of consciousness, superior to sensations, thoughts, emotions and will. The awakening of will power introduces the discovery of the Self, but if we reflect upon ourselves, if we study ourselves, we discover in our consciousness something that is not entirely our own and that betrays a spiritual origin. This we call *inspiration*.

Inspiration reveals to us a will higher than our own, a spiritual reality wider than the world of our sensations and thoughts. If we cultivate inspiration, we are led to another great discovery, similar to the discovery of the Self, which transcends the narrowness of our intellectual, emotional and volitional experience. It is the experimental discovery of God, fully achieved in the state of mystic ecstasy.

Such a real knowledge of God, which is the result of actual personal experience, must be distinguished from blind faith in God, as taught by religious teachers, who can only give to others the results of their own personal experience without enabling them to repeat that experience. Such a mystic experience transforms spiritualism so much that it produces a fifth stage in the quest for truth, called *mysticism*. Spiritualism admitted God as a result of reasoning, and defined Him as the Highest Being. If spirits are the only reality and are unequal, there must be a highest Spirit. If everything has a cause, there must be a first cause. If every law depends on a lawgiver, the laws of nature and the laws of the spirit must have a supreme source in a personal lawgiver of the highest rank. If the idea of a perfect Being exists in our thought it must correspond to a reality, for perfection implies existence.

But God as the highest Spirit, or as the first cause, or the supreme lawgiver, or the perfect Being, is not such a living reality as the God revealed to the mystic in ecstasy. Mystic experience is rarer even than a trained human will. But mysticism is the looked-for conciliation of pantheism and spiritualism; it maintains the unity of the universe insisted upon by the pantheists, and at the same time the reality of the Self discovered by the spiritualists.

As in pantheism the materialistic or the idealistic factor may prevail, so in mysticism we notice the predominance of either pantheism or spiritualism. Genuine ecstasy is an intimate union of two distinct beings, creature and Creator, the soul and God, and despite their union the consciousness of distinctness remains. But there is also a spurious pantheistic ecstasy in which this distinctness is obscured.

The contrast of these two kinds of mysticism is manifest in two great religions, Brahmanism and Christianity. Christian mystics insist on the difference between God and man, while Brahmanists insist on their identity. We cannot be surprised that the older religion corresponds to an earlier stage in the quest for truth. Spiritualism is the philosophy of Christianity, in opposition to pantheism, which is the philosophy of Brahmanism and Buddhism. In Christian mysticism we find the second synthesis of two extremes, which can obviously be accepted and understood only by the highest rank of thinkers.

Materialism, idealism, pantheism, spiritualism and mysticism correspond to the five chief types of theasy, and every conception that has ever been consistently formulated in the history of human thought fits into this classification. We might have reached the same result by starting from the history of philosophy, and classifying theasies as they have occurred, grouping the philosophers around certain representative men. Thus we should call materialism the philosophy of Democritus, idealism the philosophy of Plato, pantheism the philosophy of Parmenides, spiritualism the philosophy of Descartes, mysticism the philosophy of Plotinus.

Philosophical writers, however, may be inconsistent, and the logical alternatives which follow from the psychological analysis of consciousness are not always clear to individual thinkers, so that in the same writer we may find elements of different theasies. Chemistry isolates pure elements that are not found in nature, and every mineral is a mixture of elements. Similarly psychology isolates the pure types of theasy which may not always be found in a perfectly pure form in the actual thinkers known to history. Still, this classification has a peculiar value, as it enables us to appreciate individual thinkers and to understand the history of thought. The main currents of history are in accord with the ideal succession of the chief theasies, so that history justifies such a psychological classification.

A thinker who knows himself well enough to distinguish in his own consciousness sensations and thoughts which are his own, from inspirations coming from above, reaches the conclusion that the universe is not limited to the four classes of things which we know best as minerals, vegetables, animals and men, but that religious tradition is correct in its conception of hierarchies of spirits extending up to the highest level of Divinity. If man acts upon the inferior classes—shaping minerals, cultivating plants, and training animals—he must also admit the possibility of being acted upon by higher beings and initiated by them into a life superior to ordinary human life.

Inspiration is an objective reality of which the highest stage was long ago named *ecstasy* by the Greeks. A great number of thoroughly reliable witnesses testify to the reality of this intercourse between man and God.

Not every geographer has visited Timbuctoo, but nobody doubts its existence. The number and quality of witnesses to the reality of ecstasy, whom we call mystics, far exceeds the number and quality of explorers of Central Africa. There is therefore no reason to exclude ecstasy from psychology because few psychologists have experienced it. We accept in geographical exploration the testimony of a single reliable witness as sufficient, while all mystic states have been experienced by many witnesses who agree remarkably among themselves.

The materialism or idealism of most psychologists has prevented them from attaining a thorough understanding of inspiration, which they have often confounded with feeling or emotion, whereas inspiration is something incomparably higher, in the same way that mysticism is a higher stage than pantheism. Just as ideas are understood by reason, so inspirations are seized by intuition, which is a higher cognitive faculty. Just as we test the validity of our ideas by applying them to the understanding of our sensations, experiment being the test of every theory, so we have to test our intuitions by reasoning, which is the most universal human faculty. We have to understand our intuitions by fitting them into the general scheme of reality as represented by reason.

The knowledge of reality proceeds at three different levels: perception, thought and intuition. At each higher level we utilise the experience of lower levels, just as in ascending a ladder we use the lower rungs in order to climb higher. Reason utilises perceptions and verifies inferences by experiment; similarly intuition does not abolish reason, but uses it for the verification of its own insight. Reason is the special faculty of man, and he knows best how to use it, while intuition is an angelic faculty which is only beginning to appear in human life. It ought not to be identified, as often happens, with animal instinct, which produces the right action in animals without giving them any kind of knowledge, whereas intuition is a truly cognitive faculty, producing knowledge not inferior to that implied by thought or reasoning, both in subjective certainty and in objective validity.

In order to distinguish genuine intuition—the channel for divine inspirations—from false intuition, grasping at suggestions inspired by perverse spirits, reason is indispensable, and all the great mystics have liked to argue about their mystic experience, testing its provenience by reasoning. The abundance of false inspirations led the French spiritualist, Ernest Naville, who sincerely confessed that he had never had any mystic experience, to place mysticism among the negative philosophies, destructive of reason, instead of recognising mysticism as the supreme and ultimate achievement of spiritualism.

The consistent spiritualist is naturally led to mysticism, if he trains his will, for he easily discovers that omnipotence is possible only in harmony with a superior Will which is called Grace, or the Will of God.

In order to explain the historical fact that mysticism is apparently older than modern spiritualism (for Plotinus as early as the third century of our era was already a mystic), we must take into consideration the spiritualism of later Platonism, which must have had an influence on Plotinus, though it has scarcely been noticed by modern readers of Plato.

There was a pantheistic mysticism in Greece, Persia and India which it is not easy to distinguish from the genuine mysticism of Christianity, and this explains why feeling has often been identified with inspiration. Feeling or emotion is the basis of pantheism, while genuine inspiration, very different from feeling, is the foundation of mysticism. The love of unity, the devotion to the whole, produce in certain pantheists states of feeling similar to mystic ecstasy. But the real test of genuine ecstasy is the perfectly clear awareness of the infinite distance between creature and Creator, despite their most intimate conjunction.

Genuine ecstasy is the union of two distinct beings, and all the Christian mystics insist on that aspect of their ecstasy. Therefore mysticism, though apparently resembling pantheism in the conception of the perfect unity of the universe, establishes this unity in a living personal God who has created the universe and is distinct from all creation.

The true mystic is not a part of or an emanation from his Creator, but knows himself as a creature, and the joy of union is intensified by the consciousness of the abyss originally separating creature and Creator, which is now miraculously crossed.

The wrong identification of feeling with inspiration, of pantheism with mysticism, has discredited mysticism in the minds of many spiritualists who have been fully aware of the superiority of will over feeling, but have not been able clearly to conceive the superiority of divine inspiration over human will-power.

A true mystic has plenty of common-sense and is thoroughly practical. When he emerges from ecstasy, he has an increased lucidity, enabling him to understand actual conditions and to take an active share in life. Quietism is a pantheistic aberration rightly condemned by the Church. The intuitive experience of God, and the action of grace, cannot obscure the splendour of reason, nor weaken the power of will. Quite the contrary; the mystic has a perfectly lucid reasoning power and an indomitable will.

When the whole world was dazzled by the material power of a terrible aggression, it was a mystic and an ascetic, Cardinal Mercier, who found in his prayers and inspirations a force of resistance which surprised the world. In the life of mystics we often notice examples of sound business capacity; for instance, Plotinus was the guardian of many orphans, administering with great prudence their fortunes entrusted to his care. When the Catholic Church was crippled by the captivity of the Popes at Avignon, it was a mystic virgin, Catherine of Siena, who brought the Pope back to Rome. When France was overrun by the English, another mystic virgin crowned the king and expelled the enemy. Many such examples could be quoted: whoever studies the true mystics finds ample evidence that ecstasy does not render practical life more difficult, but furnishes serviceable inspirations that enable the mystics to accomplish tasks which had been deemed impossible.

Mysticism is an enlarged spiritualism: the experience of intimate contact with the Creator transforms the individual even more profoundly than the discovery of the soul, which makes him fully conscious of his immortality and of his freedom. While for the spiritualist, individual spirits are the only reality, the mystic finds that neither matter, nor ideas, nor the universe, nor the infinity of spirits, constitutes absolute reality, but the link of each spirit with his Creator, or the flow of divine grace. Grace is the reality of the mystic, and he considers himself real in proportion to the grace that he is able to receive.

We find philosophic mysticism in the works of Plotinus, of St Augustine, of Saint-Martin, and to a certain extent also in Malebranche, and in the latest writings of Maine de Biran. The boundary between spiritualism and mysticism is not always clearly defined, because these two theasies have much in common, and we might give to both the name of pluralism, in opposition to the monism of materialists, idealists and pantheists.

Perfect consistency in a thinker requires very rare qualities: complete disinterestedness, the love of truth above everything, the absence of vanity, of ambition, of fear, hate or anger against his adversaries. Every living man is placed in certain surroundings that influence him: they dim and distort his vision of reality. Rare force of character is necessary to resist all these influences and the personal motives which bias judgment.

Perfect wisdom depends as much on moral conditions as on intellectual capacities. In special scientific research these moral conditions are not so important, and one can be an eminent astronomer or chemist without any exceptional moral eminence. It is totally otherwise in philosophy, and above all in metaphysics. Whoever wishes to form a conception of universal existence, will not attain truth without virtue. Moral perfection is an indispensable condition for the manifestation of the highest intellectual capacities. A philosophical work intended to present a conception of life and existence depends not only on the intelligence or erudition of the author, but on the circumstances in which that work was conceived and executed, and also on the moral character of the author, on the liberty of mind which enables him to recognise his errors or to incur undeserved blame.

If an author lives among people whose convictions are opposed to his views, he will, unless he possesses a very exceptional strength of character, make concessions in order not to wound his readers; even Descartes did not dare to be perfectly sincere in his published works. The same thing also happens nowadays, when many authors make concessions to prevailing prejudice, not daring to say all that they think.

These considerations explain the difficulties of classifying authors or their works according to the general scheme of the five conceptions of existence. This general scheme, like any other theory, can only be applied to concrete reality with certain reservations. The astronomer calculates the position of a star according to the law of gravity, and his observation later shows that star in a slightly different position, due to unforeseen error caused by the imperfection of his instruments or his calculations. The chemist determines the atomic weight of an element according to the law of periodicity, and experiment gives the real atomic weight, which differs from that expected.

Nature never offers perfectly pure elements, but always mixtures; and even exceptionally pure metals, like gold or mercury, are not what is called chemically pure.

Therefore it is not surprising that pure and consistent materialism in philosophy is as rare as pure iron in metallurgy. Nor can pure and consistent idealism or pantheism be more frequent. Spiritualism is very often tinged with pantheism or idealism. Pure and consistent mysticism is rarer still.

The psychological classification retains its usefulness and corresponds to truth. It is true beyond every possible doubt that the chief contents of human consciousness are sensations, ideas, emotions, volitions and inspirations. It is also certainly true that a man in whom sensations prevail will be inclined to materialism, and a man who rejoices in abstract thought will be prone to idealism. It is equally certain that the predominance of emotions leads to pantheism. We cannot deny the peculiar experience of the discovery of one's own soul, after which it becomes impossible to doubt one's immortality or freedom. Finally, the greatest certainty of all is the fact that the intuitive knowledge of God in genuine ecstasy intensifies all faculties, enlightening the reason and strengthening the will.

The above sketch of the essential alternatives of metaphysical conception is, like every other philosophical work, an outcome of the moral, intellectual and spiritual experience of the author,[1] who has in very fact lived through all the stages he indicates, and has devoted more than forty years to the study of his predecessors in philosophy. He is humbly grateful for the privilege of having enjoyed both the leisure and vitality necessary to the pursuit of these arduous studies, and further for a certain quality of character which has enabled him to be, in a sense, independent of the limiting influences of period, environment, or, in short, of any motive other than the passionate love of truth.

[1] An account of this personal experience may be found in the author's *World of Souls* (1924), pp. 13–22. Whoever wants to understand fully the above chapters on Spiritualism and Mysticism ought to read the preceding two English volumes of the author: *The World of Souls*, published in 1924 by Allen and Unwin, and *Pre-existence and Reincarnation*, published by the same firm in 1928.

CHAPTER XIV

Final Synthesis

There is a natural sequence of efforts in the quest for truth, and the successive theasies rise gradually from materialism to mysticism. Idealism is a reaction against materialism, and pantheism is the first synthesis of opposites. Spiritualism is a reaction against pantheism, and the long struggle between the pagan pantheistic monism and Christian pluralistic spiritualism ends in a second synthesis, that of mysticism, which may well seem final.

But at this higher stage we once more see a conflict and an opposition between two opposites, similar to the first opposition between materialism and idealism, which ended in pantheism, and to the second opposition between pantheism and spiritualism, which ended in mysticism. Twice has the struggle between two opposed points of view led to a reconciliation at a higher stage. The third contrast is between the man of will and the man of God, between the spiritualist and the mystic. We may now ask, does not this third conflict also lead to a synthesis and reconciliation which would be the final outcome of all philosophy?

The conflict and contrast between the two higher types of pluralism exists, and corresponds to the old conflict between Church and state, pope and emperor. The emperor may be humiliated and brought to Canossa, or he may imprison the pope in Avignon or Fontainebleau, as was done in 1309 by Philip IV, and in 1811 by Napoleon.

What has happened on a large scale in history repeats itself in individual consciousness. Our will often resists inspiration, and sometimes inspiration overwhelms the will. The man of will is likely to look down upon the humble servant of God who renounces his own will and seeks to know the will of God in order to fulfil it. The mystic is likely to condemn the pride or selfishness of the man of will.

The outlook on reality of these two types differs, and this difference produces the two distinct theasies known as spiritualism and mysticism. In order to justify the conception of mysticism as a synthesis of spiritualism and pantheism, we had to discover a new element in consciousness, differing from *feeling*, which leads to pantheism, and from *will*, which is the basis of spiritualism. If we wish to transcend mysticism, we must find another element in human consciousness, distinct from will and inspiration, yet capable of controlling them and of using them for a higher purpose.

This new element is not likely to exist in all souls, for even intensity of will is not yet universal, and inspiration is known to still fewer individuals than will. It is difficult to name that new reality which manifests itself in a few privileged beings, and becomes in them a ruling power, controlling inspiration, will, emotions, thoughts and sensations.

We find it in exceptional men who devote their lives entirely to one purpose or mission, creating a peculiarly intimate link between themselves and their followers or companions, and forming a group of souls akin to one another. The first group of such a kind was the Christian Church, united by the love of Christ into one body, so that the life of each member belonged to the whole. Such union between individuals is the work of love, but of a transcendent love which has no name. Let us call it *active love*, thus distinguishing it from feelings and emotions of a lower and more limited description. Active love grows out of inspiration, if mystic intuition (a cognitive faculty, which reveals to us the supreme reality, our Creator, as distinct from his creatures) is applied to other objects less intensely active than God, producing a less profound impression, but on the other hand nearer to us, resembling us more closely, and therefore more easily approached.

Mystic intuition, applied to our neighbours, will enable us to distinguish the fundamental varieties of souls, particularly among those most akin to ourselves. That mystic union, such as is experienced between creature and Creator, is also possible between creatures of like nature, who establish mystic links

141

between themselves and with their Creator simultaneously, as a child may include in the same love its brothers, sisters and parents. Such a group would live on inspiration, drawn from infinite wisdom.

The first example of such a group was the Christian Church, and, within the Christian Church, the various congregations, which formed distinct communities united by active love. This active love controls individual will and utilises inspiration for the fulfilment of some mission entrusted by Providence to the particular group so formed. The linked life of a group of brethren is intermediate between the life of the spiritualist, fulfilling his own will, and the life of the mystic, fulfilling God's will.

The link is provided by that particular inspiration which is called a mission. Each individual may have a mission, but if he belongs to a genuine group, he shares his mission with the other members of that group, and the contrast between spiritualism and mysticism disappears in a higher theasy which has been called *Messianism*.

The Messianist is the man of active love, and as the most intimate groups of souls are called nations, the active love of the Messianist becomes national consciousness. We may distinguish it from all kinds of emotions or feelings, as being eminently active and creative.

A good term for this new element of consciousness would greatly simplify our argument, leading up to a definition of that ultimate synthesis of opposites which is the highest possible conception of life and being. Active love unifies human will with divine inspiration; it implies a *good* will, following the inspired revelation of our mission in the group to which we belong. If this group is a nation, its mission is closely related to a territory destined by Providence for that nation, and therefore the Messianist directs his attention to material things more than the mystic.

While the mystic in his ecstasy enjoys a certain consciousness of the other world, the Messianist loves his own country in which he has to fulfil his mission. Patriotism, or the love of one's country, is a practical consequence of the active love of one's nation. The Messianist looks at the world as a full harmony of nations, each owning a country, and each having a mission to fulfil for the benefit of the whole of mankind.

The awakening of national consciousness, or the active love of a group, is the third great discovery which transforms man essentially, the others being the experimental discovery of the soul and the experimental discovery of God. The discovery of the nation, which is intermediate between that of God and of the soul, reconciles the opposite types of the man of will and the man of God. The man of will finds an unselfish aim, the man of God a continuous flow of inspiration; and both maintain a vivid consciousness of the Self and of God. The consciousness of a mission links us with God, and the consciousness of ourselves links us with men of kindred inspirations.

It is sad to be alone, but the nation to which we belong gives us companions with whom we can fulfil a mission common to us and to them. The man who has discovered his own soul is a spiritualist, the man who has discovered his soul and God becomes a mystic, but he who, after discovering his soul and God, discovers his nation reaches the final synthesis. Obviously we are here using the term nation in a peculiar sense, not for the sum of all the inhabitants of a country, but only for the spiritual group which is accomplishing the divine mission of that country.

Sir Francis Younghusband has recently published a very interesting book, *The Coming Country* (John Murray, 1928), in which he attempts to show how the fire of a national consciousness or active love could transform first a city, then a whole country, and finally, through that country, the whole world. He says of this coming country: 'We may safely forecast that it will be that one which first sees the significance of the inner craving for spirituality—the country which first dares to put religion in the forefront of its activities, above politics, and above business, and first ventures to use its laity, as well as its clergy, and its women, as well as its men, in the direction of its spiritual life; to put spiritual above intellectual education; and to regard the home as above the school or the church in the upbringing of children. The coming country may be Russia, her soul purified and strengthened by her awful sufferings. It may be Poland, who already has the idea of a Messianic mission....It may be India, the very birthplace of great religions. It may be the Puritan-founded states of America—though they are now badly handicapped by their riches. Or it may be England—if only she will find her soul. Whichever country it may be, it will be scorned at the time. The better is always spurned by the good. And it will need a sublimer heroism and a steadier nerve than even war demands. But in the long centuries it will be hailed as the Saviour of the world and adored above all others'.

The above prophetic words, written by the famous explorer in June 1928, in the preface to his fascinating book, reveal him as a true Messianist.

Among Messianists there is no envy and no competition. A Polish Messianist would rejoice more to find the coming country in England *now*, than to wait centuries until Poland realised the same ideal. If any country becomes a nation-saviour, the other nations will be saved. But in each country the group of spirits who work in conformity with a genuine mission is an insignificant minority, so that the true English nation, by which is meant those who have inherited the English spirit and live accordingly, does not include one in ten thousand of the inhabitants of the British Isles.

The 'upper ten thousand', measured according to a standard of income, are a large crowd, if compared to the intellectual and spiritual *élite*, responsible for English literature, English art, English politics and English business. Though we have no means of numbering them, it is quite certain that those who create national life in any country are very few. Yet it is among these that the final theasy is being slowly elaborated, which will end the struggle between mysticism and spiritualism, by showing individuals and nations the way that leads to the Kingdom of God.

CHAPTER XV

Polish Messianism

Polish Messianism is a very peculiar intellectual, spiritual, literary and religious movement, created in Poland by several great men between 1830 and 1850. It is not the school of a single master, but the spontaneous expression of a national spirit.

It implies: (1) a conception of life and being different from all preceding philosophies; (2) a religious attitude, leading to the conciliation of Protestants and Catholics and to the reunion of all Christians in one truly Universal Church, in order to convert all pagans and to establish the religious unity of mankind; (3) a transformation of social and economic relations in the sense of peaceful collaboration of labour, capital and genius, in order to ensure general well-being and a highly accelerated production of wealth, so that all the needs of all men can be satisfied; (4) a transformation of political relations, leading to lasting peace between national states organised as members of a regenerated mankind.

The chief Polish Messianists may be divided into several groups, which are independent of each other. They are as follows:

    1. The first writer who used the term Messianism

to denote his philosophy was Joseph Maria Hoene Wroński (1778–1853). He spent more than fifty years in France after 1800, and wrote many works in French, publishing them in Paris by subscription among his followers. He devoted all his life to a philosophy based on two fundamental experiences, which he called *autocréation* and *découverte de l'absolu*, and which may be characterised as the experimental individual discovery of Self and of God, giving absolute certainty concerning the freedom and immortality of the soul and the direction of human life by Providence. Wroński wrote many mathematical and philosophical works, among which the most important is *Messianisme, ou Réforme absolue du Savoir humain* (3 vols. Paris, 1847). Many of his French works are to be found in the library of the British Museum.

2. After him the greatest philosopher of Messianism was August Cieszkowski (1817–1894), whose chief work, *Our Father*, is a philosophical interpretation of the Lord's Prayer. This work, after the publication of the first volume in 1847, remained in manuscript until after the author's death, when vols. II–IV were published by his son (1899–1906). Cieszkowski's philosophy has been introduced to Western readers in an excellent dissertation for the degree of doctor by Adam Żółtowski (München, 1904), under the title *Graf Cieszkowski's Philosophie der Tat*. An abridged translation of *Our Father* was published by

W. J. Rose, under the title *The Desire of all Nations* (The Student Christian Movement, London, 1919).

3. Under Cieszkowski's influence the great thinker and poet Zygmunt Krasiński (1812–1859) wrote his many poems. He also, like Wroński and Cieszkowski, announces a new era in the history of mankind, and the practical realisation of the Kingdom of God on earth.

4. In a totally different way the same message was given by Andrzej Towiański (1799–1878), a peculiar mystic, who from 1841 had a great influence on many of his countrymen in Paris, and later on, until his death, in Switzerland. He influenced his disciples through private conversations, and transformed the life of many Poles and of some Italians. His very interesting biography was published by Tancredi Canonico (Roma, 1895), and later by W. Szerlecka in French, under the title *Un Saint des Temps modernes* (3 vols. Paris, 1912–1917).

5. Towiański influenced the great poets Adam Mickiewicz (1799–1855), Juljusz Słowacki (1809–1849) and Seweryn Goszczyński (1801–1876). Their works contain many glimpses of a regenerated mankind, many prophecies since partially fulfilled.

6. Another group of Messianists is formed by the eminent philosophers Józef Gołuchowski (1797–1858), Józef Kremer (1806–1875), Karol Libelt (1807–1875), and Bronisław Trentowski (1808–1869).

They wrote several works in German, as well as many in Polish, so that their chief thoughts are accessible to Western readers.

7. In more recent times Messianism is represented by poets, such as Cyprjan Norwid (1821–1883) and Stanisław Wyspiański (1869–1907), and by thinkers, such as Stanisław Szczepanowski (1846–1900) and Wojciech Dzieduszycki (1848–1909). The only English books which introduce Messianism to Western readers are, besides Rose's translation of Cieszkowski mentioned above, *The World of Souls* (Allen and Unwin, 1924) and *Pre-existence and Reincarnation* (Allen and Unwin, 1928) by the present author.

The writers quoted above agree on the chief points, but none of them has given a complete outline of the doctrine of Messianism as a synthetic philosophy which is the final outcome of the whole development of human thought. This doctrine can, however, easily be formulated, as it is a consistent conception of existence, with practical applications to economic, political, religious and educational problems. An attempt at such a synthetic exposition has been made in German in the fifth volume (pp. 299–335) of the twelfth edition of Ueberweg's *Geschichte der Philosophie* (Berlin: Mittler, 1928).

The chief dogma of Polish Messianism is the immortality of true nations, each such nation being formed by certain spirits who reincarnate many times in the same national territory designed by Providence for that purpose.

A *true nation* is a group of spirits having a mission to fulfil in the life of mankind. Such a Messianic conception of the nation is totally different from the use of the word 'nation' in common speech, where it denotes a people or a race or the citizens of a state.

The biological unity between people of the same origin is material, just as is the political unity between citizens of the same state. These links are created by a common cause, which has produced a race or a state. The link between individuals forming a *true nation* is spiritual; it is the national consciousness of a mission or a common aim, in conformity with the highest inspiration.

The unity of a true nation is intermediate between the unity of Self and the unity of the universe in God. In the consciousness of a mission God is revealed, since a true mission can only be made manifest through divine inspiration. But at the same time the fulfilment of a mission requires the concordant activity of free spirits, aware of their freedom and of their voluntary sacrifice of every selfish desire that would prevent the harmony and unity of the group. Thus in national consciousness the full awareness of the individual as a real being is combined with the wider awareness of God, who is the source of inspiration.

Such a conception of a nation, as a group of spirits

with a common aim or mission, limits the number of nations to those that are true organs of God in the life of mankind. As the body of a single human being cannot have an indefinite number of limbs, so also mankind can only be served by a limited number of nations. Each true nation is formed by the assimilation of many different ethnical elements. Thus the English nation has been formed of Celts, Romans, Danes, Angles, Saxons, Normans; and the French nation of Celts, Romans, Franks, Burgundians, Goths.

A large number of different peoples or races has to be transformed through national consciousness into a small number of true nations, each entrusted by Providence with a mission. These missions, as given by God, must agree among themselves, and the crystallisation of nations out of the mass of races and peoples will lead to a lasting peace on earth. Each nation will have a national territory prepared by Providence for the fulfilment of its national task, and will therefore not desire to conquer other countries. But it takes a very long time to ascertain what are the divinely appointed frontiers within which a national life may grow.

Christianity has been so far introduced into the life of individuals by the example given in the individual life of Christ. Political and social relations remain pagan; and in order to convert nations a whole nation is needed to be a Messiah of nations.

Such a nation-Christ would introduce Christianity into its own social relations, and then into the political relations with other nations. Polish Messianists have believed that Poland would become the Messiah of nations. But the truth of Messianism, as the final outcome of human thought seeking to understand reality, does not depend on its acceptance by the nation which has received this revelation. Christianity was revealed to the Jews in Palestine; but they did not accept it, and Christianity became a Roman religion. Thus it might happen that Polish Messianism, revealed to the Poles and rejected by them, would be accepted by another nation. It is open to nations to compete for the introduction of the Christian spirit into social and political life. Whatever nation achieves it, will become the Messiah and Saviour of humanity, under the inspiration coming from the same Christ whom the Christians worship as their Lord and God.

This explanation of the place of Messianism in the logical development of the successive conceptions of existence leads to practical consequences in economic and political life. It also shows that Messianism is not an arbitrary invention of a small remote nation, but the contribution of that nation to the intellectual life of mankind, at a moment when this contribution is the logical outcome of preceding developments.

It is not any kind of propaganda that will induce the world to understand and welcome Messianism.

If the claim of the great Polish Messianists, that they bring into the life of mankind a new and valuable revelation, is just, this revelation will act in an immediate way in many individual souls all over the earth, until every human being will regard his individual life as a contribution to the mission of his nation. Then only will the realisation of Messianist ideals become possible.

We may ask whether such a transformation of the traditional material links which exist between individuals, and are derived from their common origin, into new spiritual links, which unite individuals of different origin into nations, each entrusted by Providence with a mission, would lead us towards that perfection of human life which we call the Kingdom of God on earth. Is it necessary to divide mankind into nations, instead of abolishing what are now called national differences, and insisting on the universal fraternity of men as children of one God? Such a nationalism seems to lead, as does imperialism, to strife, hate and war. But this is true of false nationalism only, which is chiefly exemplified by two great historical failures—Pan-Germanism and Pan-Slavism.

These doctrines, invented by the despotic governments who partitioned and oppressed Poland, are in every respect totally different from Messianism. According to Messianism, the mission of every true nation is to serve other nations, not to rule over them. A true nation unites many races in voluntary assimilation, as happened for centuries in Poland, in obvious contrast with the Germanisation and Russification recommended by Pan-Germanists and Pan-Slavists. A true nation is the home of liberty, as Poland was when the English Unitarians, exiles from their own country, settled at Raków in Poland and printed their English publications there in order to avoid the persecution which threatened them everywhere else. Also in Poland the Jews, persecuted in other countries, found not only liberty but special privileges.

The unity of mankind cannot be achieved otherwise than by certain instruments, or organs, which are *true nations*. The awakening of national consciousness in individuals produces, under divine guidance, such nations in a regenerated mankind. Perfect unity cannot arise in a homogeneous mass, until this rough mass becomes an organised whole consisting of definite members, like every other organism.

The first appearance of a spiritual unity formed out of individuals widely differing from each other was the creation of the Universal Church. But the link between individuals in the Church consists in their relation to God, expressed in creed and ritual. This is not the whole life of the individual.

It is only in union with many individuals of the same kind that the fullness of life can be manifested;

and this is the true national life, not as it is known now, but as it will become possible when the fire of national consciousness abolishes selfishness in all individuals and nations, so that everyone will devote all his energies to serve his nation, and through that nation the whole of humanity.

This fire of national consciousness will also abolish class distinctions and class warfare. All classes will become aware of a common aim; no competition between capital and labour will spoil social peace, since everyone will understand that neither capital nor labour is the real source of wealth. Capital is sterile without labour; but labour is equally unproductive without the genius of the inventor and the organiser. It is the inspiration of genius that is the true source of wealth; and if everyone understands this, the production of wealth can be immensely accelerated, until the needs of all will easily be satisfied.

The life of an individual in constant mystical union with others, who by their innate qualities are fit to be his most intimate friends, increases creative power, as we see whenever a group of friends with the same ideals live in close union. Friendship, sympathy, understanding, exalt the creative power, and produce a spiritual atmosphere in which the spirit thrives. A true nation permanently produces such an atmosphere for all its members, and enables them to make heroic efforts in the pursuit of universal happiness. Such a national life requires the realisation of the highest ideal in our earthly life—the progressive transformation of the earth into a part of heaven. The difference between this and the other life will gradually be overcome, and this life shaped after the pattern of the other life.

The chief metaphysical dogma of Messianism is palingenesis, consisting in the certainty of pre-existence and in the fixed determination to re-incarnate.[1] The Polish doctrine of palingenesis is independent of any tradition either of Greece or India, or of similar tendencies in French spiritism. It is the result chiefly of the discovery of the true nation as a metaphysical reality, and of the new experience of national consciousness, illuminating every detail of earthly life with the radiance of eternity.

National consciousness concerns the objective existence in this life of the eternal reality of a great mission or ideal. The full realisation of this ideal is impossible in a single life. If I love Poland with all my soul and if I wish to devote all my energies to Poland, not to the actual Poland as it is now, but to the Poland of my fairest dreams, a nation living an infinitely happy life of constant creative effort, helping all other nations towards the same happiness—then I shall have enough to do for æons on this earth.

---

[1] See the author's work *Pre-existence and Reincarnation* (London: Allen and Unwin, 1928), published also in Italian (Torino: Fratelli Bocca, 1930).

The Poland I love is a definite country between the rivers Oder and Dniepr, inhabited by my friends, whose company I need for all eternity. We shall, therefore, when our bodies are worn out, build new bodies of a similar appearance, in which we shall recognise each other in successive incarnations. These new bodies, improved in each incarnation, will become increasingly useful and efficient instruments for carrying out every plan that we have conceived.

Every failure in life will become a motive for renewed efforts in another life. This is true of love as well as of friendship. The woman loved in one life, and grown old and bodily decrepit, will be born again young and more beautiful than she has ever been, virtuous and innocent. There are infinite degrees of intimate union and mutual penetration of the souls of lovers. It is impossible to experience them all in a single incarnation. Many lives are needed to become thoroughly familiar with the nearest soul. There are many common experiences which are delightful and fascinating. Of all this infinite wealth of love-experience each couple of lovers knows only a small part. Whatever bliss they have felt together may be increased. But for that experience we need our bodies, since we love both the soul and the body of the beloved. Therefore we must return to this life many times, until we have penetrated all the mysteries of love.

There is a higher happiness in moral perfection or

sanctity; here again the narrow limits of one single life are quite insufficient. The stages leading from the condition of those who cannot abstain from sin, to the happy perfection of one who cannot sin at all, cannot be traversed in one life only. And when the summit is reached, when the working of miracles begins, there is so much to do, that a saint who loves his nation will renounce his own eternal bliss in heaven in order to work steadily at bringing heaven to earth for the benefit of all.

In order to do this we also need genius. Genius has rarely been united with sanctity; but the ideal of Messianism is a generation of saints who would be at the same time men of genius.

To reach this perfection even more lives are necessary than to achieve perfect sanctity. And as the individuals ascend towards perfection, the difficulty increases of raising all others to the level attained by the pioneers. This human life, which appears to us now chiefly as a succession of individual failures, will afford more and more opportunities for splendid victories of the spirit over the flesh.

Mystics have usually represented the other life as totally different from this life, and they have grown less and less interested in all that belongs to this life. Messianists love this life and they wish to improve it by introducing into every material detail the beauty of spiritual perfection. Messianism is a mysticism which utilises the very widest experience of the other life in this our earthly human life, in order to make it happy and perfect.

This Messianic happiness and perfection cannot easily be expressed in words before it is translated into acts. This explains why Messianism was created chiefly by poets and subsequently endorsed by thinkers interpreting inspiration. The reality of the new experience of national consciousness cannot be made manifest by words or arguments to those who have not experienced it. Words can only proclaim that such a sublime reality exists, that it works already in many souls, and that it will transform human life according to the promise contained in the Lord's Prayer.

Millions of Christians are praying for the Kingdom of God, for the fulfilment of God's will on earth as in heaven; and from Poland comes the glad tidings that these prayers, continued for nineteen centuries, begin at last to have an effect, producing a new kind of happiness, which seems everlasting.

Among all objects of passionate love the true nation is the greatest, since it includes everything else. The love of a life-partner and the children born of a perfectly happy marriage is one aspect of the love of our nation, since we cannot imagine a better use for their energies than in perfecting national life. The love of truth and beauty is also included in complete and perfect national life, since this implies the discovery of every truth and the creation of every beauty.

That each human spirit belongs by nature to a particular choir and can best fulfil its destiny in that choir; that the number of such choirs is limited; and that all races and peoples are only rough material for the final constitution of mankind into such *true choirs or nations*—this is the most important message given to mankind by Polish Messianism. But it can be understood and accepted only by those who have a personal experience of such an intimate union with a choir of essentially friendly spirits, even if they do not identify that choir with a nation. It may be a religious community, or a secular organisation which creates intimate spiritual links between its members. This prepares them for a wider union such as is afforded by a national mission to fulfil. This message will be welcome to them as it is an objective justification of their deepest and strongest feelings, which are condemned and ridiculed by all those who do not share them.

Now there has been from the earliest times a conflict between the monism of ancient philosophers and the pluralism of ancient religions. This conflict continues in the modern world as the opposition between a shallow and superficial internationalism, engineered by mere intelligence without any genuine inspiration, and the warm creative life of true nations, which through the fulfilment of their missions leads to a higher unity of mankind. The most intense love of one's nation does not at all exclude the love of mankind as a whole, in which that nation has its proper place. Nations are the necessary organs of the body of mankind, and the term *nationalism* has been often misunderstood and wrongly used in the same misleading way as spiritualism is used for spiritism, idealism for spiritualism. That wrong nationalism is imperialism, a source of strife, while true nationalism is a condition of lasting peace among the nations.

This true nationalism differs from soulless imperialism, as freedom from universal slavery. In the struggle between Christianity and materialistic, soulless and godless Socialism, Polish Messianism appears as the latest succour of Christianity, not only against modern premature internationalism, but also in the world-wide competition with older pantheistic religions such as Buddhism and Brahmanism, and with the later great religious movement of Islam, which is the most serious rival of Christianity.

Messianism has been called a philosophy of action; and indeed it has more immediate applications to practical life than have the great philosophies which have preceded Polish national thought—materialism, idealism, pantheism, spiritualism and mysticism. The Messianist is a mystic who takes a most active part in the material organisation of life. He is more often a leader of industry or a working man, an artist or an educator, than a mere theorist, a thinker or a writer.

Messianism penetrates the practice of life, and it will take a very long time before the philosophy of Messianism is worked out in detail as the Greek philosophies of materialism, idealism and pantheism, or the French philosophy of spiritualism, have been.

It is not a merely theoretical doctrine which can easily be translated from one language into another, but it is chiefly a peculiar attitude towards life as a whole, adopted by many individuals who are united in a common endeavour. Ages of this new experience in common will be necessary before the total amount of inspiration received by one nation can become available for the benefit of all other nations.

CHAPTER XVI

Palingenesis and Christianity

As Messianism is the outgrowth of Christianity, the attempt to introduce Christianity into social and political relations, and as it implies palingenesis, which is often supposed to be condemned by the Church as incompatible with other dogmas, we have to consider this apparent contradiction before Messianism can be accepted by all Christians.

As a matter of fact, reincarnation has never been condemned by the Church, and pre-existence was condemned only in the particular form set forth by Origen and Priscillian, and this nearly fourteen centuries ago. Since the sixth century there has never been any condemnation of pre-existence or of reincarnation. This silence of the Church is more significant than the silence of the mystics. There have been many opportunities for a public declaration by the Church on this subject, as many unimportant heresies have been condemned, and the popular propaganda of palingenesis in the nineteenth century grew stronger than ever.

It is really not the Church which is against palingenesis, but only a considerable portion of the clergy, who oppose it for purely professional reasons, very similar to those which led to the clerical aversion to Copernicus in the sixteenth century and to Darwin in the nineteenth.

Two theories, the one astronomical and the other biological, were fiercely attacked by the clergy, but neither was in express terms formally condemned by the Church. Nowadays we see a metaphysical theory similarly provoking the hostility of the clergy, but not incurring the explicit anathema of the Church.

In all three cases the reason is the same. These theories are alike in the following respects: first, they are not easy to justify fully, so that they require intellectual effort and an open mind in order to perceive their real agreement with the established dogma; and secondly, they deprive preachers of the easiest method of influencing their flock, by the fear of immediate punishment after death. At higher spiritual levels the thought of reincarnation acts as an inducement to strenuous efforts in order to train for a really better life. But barbarians, if they hear of another incarnation, make this an excuse for persistence in sin and postponement of conversion. That is why Augustine, who in his youth admitted reincarnation as an evident truth, like all educated people of his age, had to give it up when he became a bishop among the barbarians. He found that in order to improve them he had to frighten them by the immediate prospect of hell, without any hope of a future opportunity for repentance and reform.

This attitude of Augustine has become predominant among the clergy of all Christian denominations since the invasion of the barbarians who destroyed the Roman Empire.

Poland is the chief home of the doctrine of reincarnation, because it has not, like France, England, Italy and Spain, been overwhelmed by barbarians since the fourth century. When at last in the eighteenth century the barbarians partitioned Poland, the nation was already formed. The nineteenth century witnessed a new and a worse invasion of barbarians from within, through the advent of modern democracy, socialism and bolshevism, which give political power to uneducated masses. But in course of time these new barbarians will be educated, and when they have learned to control their animal passions, they will be able to return to divine sonship and to understand the great promise of Christ (John xiv, 12): 'Verily, verily, I say unto you, he that believeth on me, the works that I do shall he do also; and greater works than these shall he do'.

Nothing corresponds more fully to this prediction than the realisation on earth, in human life, of the loftiest hopes of angelic and celestial bliss. But this can only be won by frequent returns to this earth of each soul devoted to the service of mankind. Many of the opponents of palingenesis contend that it contradicts the New Testament. But it is easy to show that many passages of the New Testament may be interpreted as evidence for the familiarity of the disciples of Christ with the idea of reincarnation.

They thought that Christ might be a reincarnation of Elijah, Jeremiah or another prophet, and our Lord did not deny such a possibility (Matt. xvi, 14; Mark viii, 28; Luke ix, 8, 19). He said Himself that Elijah was reincarnated as John the Baptist (Matt. xi, 14; xvii, 12; Mark ix, 12). He said that whosoever forgoes home, brothers, parents, wife or children in the service of God, will regain all these a hundredfold (Matt. xix, 28, 29; xx, 16; Mark x, 29–31; Luke xviii, 29–34); and there is no possible explanation for the fulfilment of this promise other than reincarnation, as nobody can marry in a single life a hundred times, and not every servant of God having lost home or wife for the sake of God finds them again in this life. Even the term of palingenesis is used in that connection (Matt. xix, 28), and its meaning is obviously the same always: it means rebirth and nothing else. To deny this one must be strongly prejudiced.

Also such sayings as that the first shall be last and the last first (Luke xiii, 30; Matt. xix, 30; Mark x, 31, 43), or that whosoever loses his life for the sake of Christ shall regain it (Matt. x, 39; Mark viii, 35; Luke ix, 24; xvii, 33; John xii, 25), cannot well be explained otherwise than by a plurality of lives. To lose one's life means death, and to regain it means birth. Changes from first to last, and the reverse, are not frequent in a single life, but they are very probable in a succession of lives.

The most evident allusion to palingenesis is contained in the conversation of Christ with Nicodemus (John iii, 3–13), though even this has been explained away by another interpretation. Christ says clearly to Nicodemus: 'Except a man be born anew, he cannot see the Kingdom of God'. Nicodemus asks whether a man can be born when he is old, and Christ answers that a man must be born 'of water and of the Spirit', which might be interpreted as the double influence of bodily heredity and spiritual pre-existence on each individual destiny. If we understand water in the sense of matter, like Thales, then rebirth of water and the Spirit would mean the material descent of the body from certain ancestors and the spiritual growth of the soul through past incarnations. Jesus rebukes Nicodemus because he pretends not to understand, and He adds: 'No man hath ascended into heaven, but he that descended out of heaven'. This is a clear reference to the return to incarnate life after a span of eternal rest.

Also the plain promise of Christ, that we shall obtain everything for which we pray (Matt. vii, 7; Mark xi, 24), has no real meaning unless we relive our human life, to which most of our prayers refer, as they contain demands realisable only in human conditions. If a man prays throughout a long life for the possession of a home, in which he may live free from material anxiety, and if he does not attain this desire in his present life, it is evident that he must be born again as an incarnate soul in order that the promise given to him by Christ in the Gospel may be fulfilled.

Many such prayers of devout believers are not fulfilled in their lifetime and can be fulfilled only in a similar human life, as they refer to our earthly needs; for instance, perfect health, pecuniary independence, or some definite improvement in the conditions and institutions of society. If everything which is persistently prayed for is to be given, then all those things for which we pray without any visible effect in this life must be given to us in another similar life, and that cannot happen without a new incarnation.

Many things prayed for have a meaning and an importance only for an incarnate spirit, and therefore this spirit must become incarnate again in order to receive them. Thus faith in palingenesis is inevitable if we trust Christ's word that He will keep His great promise, which is not yet realised and credited by the majority of Christians.

Also, when the disciples ask Christ whether a man born blind is punished for his sins (John ix, 1), they imply pre-existence, and Christ does not deny it. His own pre-existence, though not in a human body, was clearly affirmed when He said that David worshipped Him as his Lord (Matt. xxii, 44; Mark xii, 37;

Luke xx, 44). When He says that God is the God of the living and not of the dead, and that Abraham, Isaac and Jacob are alive (Matt. xxii, 31–32; Mark xii, 26–27; Luke xx, 37–38), this seems also to mean reincarnation, as for His contemporaries a shadowy existence in Hades would not be true life. Life to them, as opposed to death, was always the life of an incarnated soul. The saying that whoever has, shall receive (Matt. xiii, 11–12; Mark iv, 10, 25; Luke viii, 10, 18) is best explained as referring to the growth of capacities and character by personal effort towards the attainment of genius and sanctity. In this growth our own efforts are reinforced by divine grace.

These quotations from the Gospels do not exhaust all the allusions in the New Testament. They are merely examples of interpretation, which may suffice to open the eyes of some readers to a new meaning of well-known passages. Whoever accepts this new meaning will find in the Old and New Testaments many other similar passages that show that pre-existence is not at all contradictory to the Bible, and that reincarnation is clearly indicated. The only passage usually quoted as evidence against rein-carnation is in the Epistle to the Hebrews (ix, 27), where it is said that we die once (in each life) and that after death the judgment of God decides the conditions of our future existence. This is not in-consistent with an acceptance of palingenesis, as the ulterior existence after judgment might well be a new human life, and the judgment would decide the conditions of that life. In this passage the stress is laid on the fact of divine judgment, and the uniqueness of each life need not mean that there is no other. Each life is unique in its quality, and after each life there is a judgment; but it would contradict immortality to affirm that any of our lives is absolutely unique. If we are immortal there must be after this life another life and perhaps many lives, no matter whether in bodies similar to those we wear now, or in other conditions.

For anybody convinced of pre-existence it is not easy to explain why this truth is not affirmed more explicitly in the Bible, and how so many passages which seem to imply it have been for so many centuries interpreted otherwise. Some solution of these two difficulties has to be given if we wish to remain Christians and still adhere to the old dogma, confirmed in some of us by an intuitive and intimate certainty. This certainty, even without concrete reminiscence, becomes an invincible incentive to affirm that we have already lived a human life before. The relative silence of the Bible can be explained, according to the Polish seer Słowacki, by the fact that the authority of the Church among Christians was very much greater than that of any previous religious authority; therefore it might have done harm to include in the Christian teaching a truth which could be fully utilised only if discovered individually.

History has shown that this truth had a different effect according to the spiritual level of those who accepted it. At a lower level it became an excuse for adjourning self-improvement—only at a higher level it added a motive for efforts. As Christianity had to become a religion of the masses and of emancipated slaves, it was sufficient to reveal to them the incarnation of Christ, without insisting on the analogy between this unique incarnation and common reincarnation. The truth revealed in the Eleusinian mysteries to the elect was not suitable for those who had lived almost animal lives, and who were raised to human dignity through the new universal religion. They had first thoroughly to understand the facts of immortality and responsibility, and an intimation that they had prepared their own state by forgotten sins might weaken the hope of full redemption and limit the consciousness of freedom. The Christian Church had to act, in respect of pre-existence and reincarnation, just as parents do with their children when they conceal from them the truths of sexual life, which are gradually revealed as the children grow up.

This mission of the Christian Church accounts, not only for the relative silence of the Bible, but also for the bias of theologians in their interpretation of such passages which contain allusions to a truth not yet clearly proclaimed. The time for proclaiming that truth came in the nineteenth century, when the long evolution of older theasies culminated in the final synthesis of Messianism.

It is a welcome confirmation of the infallibility of the Church that reincarnation has not been expressly condemned by the Church, though so many minor errors have been dealt with in the famous Syllabus of Pius IX and in the encyclicals of the later popes. The standpoint of the Church is well stated in a private letter written by Cardinal Mercier to the author, fourteen months before his death, on December 15th, 1924. He says:

'La question que vous me soumettez est bien délicate. Je crois que l'opinion de la pré-existence et de la réincarnation, telle que vous la présentez et dont vous vous dites subjectivement persuadé, n'est pas formellement condamnée comme hérétique. Mais il est certain qu'elle va à l'encontre du sens chrétien et catholique. J'ai eu, j'ai encore égard, à votre bonne foi personnelle et ne voudrai donc pas vous accuser d'hétérodoxie pour tenir à votre opinion; mais présentée *objectivement*, je crois que la doctrine de la pré-existence et des réincarnations serait sujette à condamnation, et je ne pourrais vous autoriser à la couvrir de mon patronage, d'aucune façon.'

We see that the great scholar pays homage to historical truth, but, as the scholar is also a saint and a responsible archbishop, he is anxious not to be drawn into public discussion. That letter was written in answer to my enquiry at the time when I was preparing the third Polish edition of my treatise on immortality, and wished to include in that book two new chapters on palingenesis. I respected my eminent friend's restriction and did not mention his name in the Polish book, nor his letter in the English publication of those two chapters. But his death releases me from the above request, and the testimony of such a great scholar and saint is too important in the quest for truth to be kept private.

His declaration, that palingenesis is contrary to Christian and Catholic opinion, does not countervail his admission that it has not been condemned, and that he does not consider a Catholic who is aware of his pre-existence to be a heretic. The reluctance of the Christian clergy, both Catholic and Protestant, to admit reincarnation is sufficiently accounted for by the educative character of the Church, which has to deal with millions of rough barbarians, more likely to find, in the hope of reincarnation, an excuse for persisting in sin, than an incentive for renewed efforts to establish the Kingdom of God on earth.

CHAPTER XVII

Regenerated Mankind

If human will, assisted by divine inspiration, emancipates the whole of mankind from the consequences of the Fall which are evident in our present state, then a great transformation will be achieved of which certain features may be foreseen. It is easier to say what features of our contemporary life will disappear, than to outline the positive details of that perfect life in the Kingdom of God. Similarly, the Church rarely defines any positive dogma, but chiefly condemns various heresies.

First of all, very small states are likely to disappear, not only such as Andorra, but even such as Belgium, Holland and Switzerland. A national state requires a certain size much greater even than France and Italy combined. A national life creates a powerful movement which attracts individuals from a vast area. The first example of such an integration would be the reunion of the Latin states—France, Italy, Spain and Portugal—with the French parts of Switzerland and Belgium.

They once formed one commonwealth, and they have so much in common that all over this vast area the French language and French literature are generally known. The political union of these states would not exclude full autonomy of the separate provinces. The larger unity of a great state would have as its chief aim the administration of justice, which is often hampered by purely local considerations.

We may also expect a similar union of the Slavs around Poland and of Scandinavia with Germany, Austria, Holland and German Switzerland. This would reduce the number of European nations to four, if England with its colonies and the United States formed also one great commonwealth. China, India and Persia might become the chief nations in Asia, gathering around them peoples akin to one another.

Many of the departments of the modern state will become superfluous. Thus, public instruction is the business of private local associations, and not of the state. Also a war department would have no meaning if universal lasting peace were secured by national and international justice. The whole financial organisation for collecting taxes will become superfluous if patriotic generosity secures the steady flow of voluntary gifts to the Treasury.

The great number of officials in our modern states would be reduced to a few chosen and really efficient servants of the state for the administration of justice, foreign affairs and public order. National life is a spontaneous growth and cannot depend upon the government of the state. It needs daily creative inspiration, while the state ought to be naturally conservative, maintaining what the initiative of generations has produced. While the state comes to represent real power, social life deepens independently of that power, through private initiative. The power of the state must be limited to what is really indispensable, to what constitutes a guarantee of freedom for all citizens. Freedom implies also the liberty of educating our children according to our convictions, of forming all kinds of associations for various purposes, of carrying out all kinds of business for the advantage of our neighbours.

While small states will disappear, big cities will also become superfluous. The improvement of means of communication will allow every family to have a healthy home in the country and will organise business in each district so as to satisfy the needs of all the inhabitants. Commerce and industry have everything to gain by decentralisation, if only the products of labour can easily be transported anywhere.

When the army of tax collectors, customs officers, and soldiers disappears, everybody will be engaged in some useful production for the benefit of his nation and of mankind in general. Only important collections, museums, libraries, etc., will remain centralised and the British Museum will prove to be the most durable institution in London, when most houses around it have been pulled down and their grounds transformed into beautiful gardens with suitable dwellings for scholars and artists coming from all parts of the globe to consult the wealth of information accumulated in that venerable institution.

The growth of big cities has been caused by economic conditions of production, and particularly by difficulties of transport. When these difficulties are overcome and production spreads all over the country, then such an accumulation of population in one city will no longer be justifiable, and the capitals of future states will resemble Washington or Bern rather than London or Paris.

Decentralisation of production, a great reduction of government offices, and the transfer to voluntary local social bodies of a great amount of the present government business, will increase the importance both of private initiative and of creative genius in every department of life. The change from crowded city life to civilised and well-organised country life will create conditions more favourable to genuine inspiration and to healthy activity.

We must add also the indefinite prolongation of each individual life, and the maintenance of the body at every age in a state of perfect efficiency. Physicians will gradually disappear, and, if moral health corresponds to physical health, lawyers and clergymen will also become superfluous. These professions are unproductive, and the ideal society will consist of productive individuals.

Production may be technical, intellectual, or artistic, each home being a workshop in which some values are elaborated. Each family having a house in a garden, domestic service will become an educational practice of citizenship, as mechanical contrivances will limit to the utmost the amount of indispensable work. Food will mostly reach the homes ready for use, vegetarianism and fruitarianism becoming general, and the kitchen fire will be supplanted by electric stoves.

Not only will soldiers, tax collectors, customs officers, physicians, lawyers and clergymen have nothing to do, but working men as a class will naturally become extinct, all the work being done efficiently by cultured individuals devoting only a part of their time to production, and the rest to active participation in social life.

Such limitation of necessary work will leave more time for what, though not exactly indispensable, is yet of great value—contact with the thought of others, establishing a closer relation between the inhabitants of each district and each country than has ever before existed.

A free spirit cannot be the slave of necessary duties. He needs leisure and will have it. This leisure may be taken in different ways, either a number of hours every day, or a number of years of complete leisure after some years of intense work. Very likely this second form will prevail, as every task undertaken for public benefit by an enthusiastic worker will engage all his capacities, and for such inspired workers life will become a succession of all-absorbing tasks, giving complete satisfaction.

A nation formed of such workers will become a genuine member or organ of regenerated mankind. When the whole of humanity is organised into such happy nations, some universal tasks may be undertaken; as, for instance, the control of the climate, which will make the whole earth habitable; a central world government, ensuring lasting peace and mutual good-will among nations; organisation of interplanetary messages and even travel; modification of the movements of the earth according to human convenience.

At the highest stage of such a development the difference between this and other worlds will be abolished, and our bodies will become immortal, eternally young, so that birth, death and procreation will no longer be needed. Such a sanctified humanity will finally make this earth a part of Heaven, a world of eternal bliss. We cannot imagine nor picture the life of these redeemed descendants of our generation. Some happy moments in our present life give us glimpses of this future, and if each of us searches diligently, he will discover such moments either in his own life or in the life of others, in the waking state or in inspired dreams of a prophetic kind. A life without violence, anger, fear, hate, envy, calumny,

strife—a life full of joy, always shared with understanding friends—a life of sanctity, always aware of
divine omnipresence—a life of genius, producing
beauty without effort—this is a true vision of the
future awaiting regenerated mankind.*

* In 1910 the author published in Polish his work *Ludzkość
Odrodzona* (Regenerated Mankind), which contained a detailed
prediction of the World War and many glimpses of the future
state of mankind. During the war many chapters from this
book were reprinted in the Polish daily Press in Europe and
America, to keep up the hope of a happy end of the struggle.

CHAPTER XVIII

The Immediate Outlook

The way to the goal is so long and weary that even the humblest attempt to paint a picture of regenerated mankind may appear to most readers but an idle fancy. They will ask what can be done immediately by those who have learnt the truth and have some vision of the ultimate destiny of mankind. Is it only for Providence to act upon individuals until they awake from this cruel dream of our actual life, or can individuals in some way co-operate with Providence?

Sir Francis Younghusband suggests theatrical performances and debating societies as the first means of social action on a fallen world. But he presupposes a whole group of highly gifted individuals gathered in one place. This is not very likely to happen, unless we create conditions for the education of such persons, and therefore some kind of school seems to be the first active step needed. Even a single master, if he thoroughly understands reality and can provide the necessary means, could educate a whole group of workers, fit for any social, literary, artistic or political activity leading towards the goal.

Most existing schools have to take into account the requirements of the state, and lack the necessary independence for the production of a new type of Messianic worker. A Messianic school must equip its pupils for life, mark out for them individual tasks according to individual capacities, and help them to carry out these tasks against all odds and all kinds of prevailing prejudice.

Those workers whom Sir Francis Younghusband imagines gathered in a small city, as if by accident, must come from some spiritual home, in which they have been prepared for their difficult task. Such a school and mission centre, from which the glad certainty of the final regeneration of mankind could radiate, would require considerable means, as it would differ in many respects from any other school. It would in certain ways resemble one of those monasteries in which laymen spend a certain time for their spiritual advantage, and in order to start a new life. Our school would receive such guests for different periods, besides the permanent pupils who could be educated there from childhood.

Both children and adults would be expected to work chiefly by themselves, according to the master's indications, and the courses of study would be of a kind which only very gifted pupils could enjoy and profit by. Such an institution for the education of children and adults, with a view to the fulfilment of voluntarily accepted tasks of national importance, might be named a *Forge*. It would be a kind of laboratory for the transformation of souls, so as to make them fit for the struggle against the actual state of things in the outer world.

Another line of activity might be the publication of a weekly paper, recording contemporary life and events from the point of view of the expected Kingdom of God. General news, including reviews of books and artistic productions generally, would be presented in such a way as to lay stress on events which seem to indicate the approach of the great transformation. Books might be published for that purpose, containing the essential knowledge needed by such workers as those whom Sir Francis Younghusband mentions in his book.

General history, which usually is a very pessimistic record of human injustice, needs to be rewritten from the standpoint of the hope of regeneration. We have to find in the past indications which justify that hope, if there are any. We want to know the truth at all costs, and we are not afraid to learn the worst. Even had history taught us that mankind had always been equally cruel and unjust, or had gone from bad to worse within the last thousand years, this should not at all destroy our hope of a better future. But it is likely that if we seek carefully we shall find some encouragement in our quest. From the ordinary manuals of history we learn about kings, battles and generals, but very little about the activities of saints. Whoever is familiar with them knows that even in the worst times some exceptional individuals achieved sanctity, and such facts are more important for our purpose than great battles won or lost. Reliable biographies of saints and men of genius reveal miracles of successful endeavour undertaken and carried through in spite of enormous difficulties.

Biographical literature has been increasing throughout the nineteenth century, and this is a sign of man's ever-growing interest in the power of character. A standard library of biographies of great men written from a definite point of view would become a powerful instrument for the moral regeneration of mankind.

Apart from all our own efforts, there is a continuous action of Providence on individuals and on nations which is steadily improving the prospects of mankind. We are living in a period of transition, and the decay of much that was good in the past may sometimes blind us to the signs of better things in the future. The number of international organisations rapidly increases, and many links are formed between distant countries. In our daily life we use the products of many lands, and the co-operation of many people of different nations has been required to bring these products to our doors. Any event of importance for good or evil happening anywhere on earth awakens interest and sympathy almost everywhere.

Thus mankind grows towards unity, and daily improvements in the means of communication accelerate this progress. Such an international movement as that of Co-operative Societies started from a small town in England and went round the world.

A regular account of all these international relations, a record of all that is being done for mutual improvement, would be a great encouragement to all those who long for universal brotherhood and peace. *The Times Literary Supplement* is an instance in point. Since 1901 it has furnished a survey not only of English literature, but of all the most important books in other languages, and thus has acquired a much more international character than the analogous French *Nouvelles littéraires*, started twenty years later. It is an example of a private undertaking becoming a public institution by sheer objective usefulness. Many similar examples are sure to follow. Often an enterprise having the humblest beginnings will grow to world-wide importance, like the watch industry of Geneva.

Sir Francis Younghusband is perfectly right in saying that the thorough transformation of a single city would be the beginning of a movement embracing a whole country, and then spreading to other countries by force of the example of the first redeemed country. But the creation in some quiet place of a home for the new spirit, whence its influence might radiate all over the world, would be much easier than the task of spiritualising a whole city.

From such a Forge books and journals might come

forth and influence not only the country of their origin; missionaries of a new scholarly and scientific type might be sent out to lecture and to teach the *gay saber* of a new kind of love, linking individuals into true nations, and nations into a regenerated mankind.

Therefore the creation of a school, a modern monastery and psycho-physical laboratory, constituting a Forge, somewhere in the mountains, in a not yet too densely populated country, seems to be the very first task confronting those who accept the gospel of the possible regeneration of mankind and who wish to employ actively all their energies and to devote their lives to that purpose. In his own country the author has preached the necessity for this since the beginning of the present century; in England, it was formulated in the conclusion of the author's *World of Souls* in 1924, but as yet he has not found friends who could help him to carry out that programme. This is sufficiently accounted for by Christ's saying about the wealthy and the Kingdom of God. But if we are right, sooner or later others will be more successful in doing what we have set our heart on.

The quest for truth has led us not only to an understanding of the reality of true nations as the ultimate outcome of the age-long search, but also to a practical plan of activity which would be a vast experiment carried out on mankind, in order to test the truth of our theoretical speculations. For the general understanding of reality there is no valid test other than to live according to that understanding. The lives of the Christian saints were a test of the truth contained in the Gospels, and the life of a nation becoming aware of its mission will be the ultimate test of that most recent interpretation of the social aspects of Christianity which has been given in the philosophy of Messianism.

We do not claim more than to have given a full and correct interpretation of the Lord's Prayer. If the Kingdom of God is to come, and the will of God is to be accomplished on earth—as it is in Heaven —some way of escape from the present state of misery must exist. We need a special workshop, in which the plans of that expected Great Transformation could be prepared in detail by competent experts, and then carried out gradually in many countries.

Such an institution would acquire authority only after many years of really effective activity. The inherent contradiction in the initial conditions for founding this first Forge lies in the fact that very considerable means would be required, and the wealthy are the least receptive of such revolutionary plans. They enjoy a relative comfort and independence, which makes them generally unable to realise the misery of large majorities in all parts of the world.

We have to obtain the necessary means from those who by the fact of their wealth are not very accessible to spiritual influences. How can we expect them to give up a considerable portion of their wealth for a risky experiment which is not likely to yield immediate returns? For they could have no guarantee of witnessing the results of their sacrifice, nor of participating actively in the work for which they would supply the means.

This implies a faith which only a very exceptional Master could inspire. False prophets all over the world have produced universal distrust of any claims of spiritual mastery of an active kind. Much money has been lost through such false prophets, and therefore it will not be easy to induce those who could afford it to help in the foundation of a Forge. The only people likely to spend their money on such a risky experiment are those who have risen by their own efforts from poverty to wealth, like Mr Ford. But such persons are not at all likely to read this book, unless it wins a fame similar to that of *Alice in Wonderland*, as a work introducing the readers into a beautiful world so totally different from our own that it forms a refreshing contrast to our vulgar everyday cares.

There is a way out of these cares, not by merely dreaming about a better world, but by doing what each of us can do to improve himself and the conditions of life for his neighbour. The number of those who have decided to act in this way is rapidly increasing all over the world, according to the author's experience. They form various organisations and societies everywhere, but often lack the vision of wider horizons. If the application of metaphysics, or the knowledge of Reality, to social and political activity became as universally recognised as the application of mathematics to practical engineering, then the progress towards the goal would gain immensely in speed and efficiency.*

* On March 11, 1930 the first attempt was made in the small town of Łowicz to deliver in three days at the rate of three lectures a day a popular course of metaphysics, the contents of this volume. Five hundred persons of all classes and of every degree of education listened for three hours every day to a popular presentation of the contents of this volume. Similar courses are intended in sixty-five cities of Poland, under the management of *Polska Macierz Szkolna*, the greatest Polish educational organisation Such an experiment would have been impossible before the war. The author is ready to repeat it in Great Britain, the British Colonies and America if needed. Nothing helps better to establish peace among men of different views than such an impartial explanation of all possible alternatives in metaphysics.

INDEX

Failures, forgotten, 120; a source of hope, 158
Fall of angels and men, 68, 77, 87, 175
False prophets, 1, 189
Fanaticism, 108
Fascination of dancing, 34
Feeling and inspiration, 133
Fictions used, 95–96
Final synthesis, 6, 48, 139
Finality, prevails, 24; depends on mind, 36
Fire transforms matter, 50
Fishers and hunters, 50
Floods, 50
Fontainebleau, 140
Force of character needed by a thinker, 135
Forge, a laboratory for souls, 183, 186–189
Forgotten achievements, 120
Foundation of metaphysics, 114
France, 86, 118, 122, 166, 175
Freedom of will, 104
Freemasons, 106
French spiritualism, 120; to be distinguished from spiritism, 157
Freud, 121
Fruitarianism, 51
Fruits, how tested, 22

Gambling den, 72
Garrulity, 63
Gassendi, 12
Geneva, 186
Genius, 156, 159
Gentile, 105
German monism, 120
Germanisation, 155
Germany and France, 120

Giver of inspiration, 115
Goal of government, 59
God, 104, 109, 124, 127, 151
Gołuchowski, 149
Goszczyński, 149
Gothic cathedral, 39
Grace the reality of the mystic, 132, 134
Grass changed into corn, 51
Gratry, 119
Great Britain, 84
Great Transformation, 188
Greco-Roman imagination, 39
Greece, 86, 132, 157
Growth of ideas, 102
Gymnastics, 63

Haeckel, 13
Hamlet, 46
Hartley, 12
Hartmann, 121
Havelock Ellis, 33
Health a matter of business, 55
Healthy homes, 177
Heaven affected by the earth, 87
Hebrews, Epistle to, 170
Hedonists, 10
Hegel, 105
Hegesias, 10
Hell for barbarians, 165
Heraclitus, 8
Heredity, 67
Heresies, 164
Heroic ancestors, 88
Heroic efforts, 156
Hidden things may be real, 85
Hierarchy, of arts and sciences, 38, 45; of types, 4; of spirits, 129

195   13-2

Metaphysics, 135, 190
Metapsychics[1], 27, 40, 48, 74
Mettrie, de la, 12
Mickiewicz, 149
Microscope, 23
Miletus influenced Thales, 7
Minorities in a national state, 85
Mission reveals God, 151
Modern industry, 52
Molecules and stars, 18, 19, 21
Moleschott, 13
Monastic chastity, 66
Monastic seclusion, 68
Monism, against pluralism, 161; against religion, 113
Monists ignore themselves, 113
Moral virtue essential for a philosopher, 135
Mortification, 61
Motors, 52
Movement, explained, 102; in art, 38
Murray, 144
Music as an art, 39
Musicians worshipped as gods, 41
Mystic ecstasy when genuine, 132
Mystic experience, 127
Mystic in conflict with the spiritualist, 139
Mystic intuition applied to creatures, 66, 141
Mystical power of the soil, 88
Mysticism, spurious, 14; genuine, 126, 131, 139; transcended, 140

Mystics and Messianism, 159

Napoleon, 140
Nation-Christ, 153
Nation defined, 80, 151
National activity transforms a country, 81
National consciousness, abolishes classes, 156; is active love, 142
National life, 79, 83, 87
National mission an eternal reality, 157
National territory, 152
Nationalism misunderstood, 162
Nations, as definite members of humanity, 155; number of, 152
Natural conditions of life modified, 52
Natural frontiers, 84
Naturalists, their bias, 13
Naville, 3, 6, 119, 131
Necessity mechanical and logical, 98
Negation of spirit, 96
Negative discipline, 61, 64
New Thought, 111
Nice, 86
Nicodemus, 168
Norwid, 150
Nothingness, how produced, 112
Number applied to matter, 95

Objectivity of an unuttered poem, 45

[1] The term metapsychics was introduced by the author in 1902 in his Polish work *Poprzednicy Platona*, Kraków, 1902, p. xxiii. Much later it was adopted by Charles Richet.

[1] The term *psychema* has been introduced and justified by the author in his French work *Volonté et Liberté*, Paris, 1913, pp. 36–39.

Reincarnation never condemned, 164
Relativity of matter, 69
Relics, 70, 71
Religion, 1, 144
Religious attitude of the Messianist, 147
Religious communities, 161
Religious dogma, 103, 119
Religious indifference, 111
Religious unity of mankind, 147
Renouvier, 2, 3, 119
Representation of plays instructive, 47
Republic of Plato, 99
Respiratory exercises, 63
Reunion of Christians, 147
Revelation, 115, 154
Rhymes and rhythms, 42
Rhythm and measure of sounds, 39
Richet, 198
Ritual, 14, 69, 70
Romans, 152
Rome, 73
Rose, 149, 150
Rule of the struggle against temptations, 63
Russia, 145
Russification, 155

Sacraments, 75, 76
Safety from enemies, 55
Saint-Martin, 135
Sanctification, 92, 96
Sanctity reached through many lives, 159, 185
Saviour, 145, 153
Savoy, 86
Scandinavia, 176
School of messianic workers, 182

Science, 14, 16, 60, 90, 114
Scorn of the coming country, 145
Scott, 3
Sculpture, 29–32, 36
Secrétan, 119
Sectarians, 106
Seer differs from the thinker, 115
Sensations, 41, 60
Sensualism, 14
Sex, new theory of, 65
Sexual life, 65, 67, 68, 91
Shakespeare, 46
Signature, its value, 54
Silence of the Church and of the mystics on reincarnation, 164
Simplification of use resulting from complicated tools, 53
Size of electrons, 95
Skill of commercial transactions, 54
Skilled distribution of wares, 49
Slaves of the body, 61
Slavs around Poland, 176
Słowacki, 149, 171
Small states, 177
Smell and taste, 21
Smith, Adam, 14
Socialism, 14, 166; against Christianity, 162
Soil, object of love, 88; source of inspiration, 82
Soldiers, 55
Sophistes of Plato, 100
Soul has no visible form, 103
Sound is material though invisible, 39
Sounds, are real, 26; are subtler matter than stars or electrons, 45

INDEX

INDEX

Training of will power, 60, 63,
91
Transformation, of material
environment, 75; of social
relations, 147
Transmission of news, 53
Transubstantiation, 76, 78, 80,
91, 95
Treasury, 176
Trentowski, 149
Tribal selfishness destroyed,
84
Triumph of the spirit, 71
True Being, 1, 6, 116, 123
True nations, 155
Types of men, 81, 97
Tyranny, 108

Ueberweg, 150
Ultimate solution of the prob-
lem of matter, 93
Upper ten thousand, 146
United States, 176
Unity, of Being, 109; of man-
kind, 185
Universal Church, 147
Universal fraternity, 154
Universal happiness, 156
Unphilosophic country, 118
Unspoken poems, 43
Unspoken words and verses,
42
Utilitarianism, 13

Vacherot, 119
Valéry, 33, 35, 63
Validity of ideas, 130
Valla Laurentius, 11
Vegetarianism, 51
Venice, 86
Victory of the spirit, 75, 159
Violin, 40

Visual scheme of matter, 18
Vitalism, 27
Vogt, 13
Voluntary procreation, 67

War Department, 176
Ward, 3, 121
Washington, 178
Water as a symbol of heredity,
168
Wave a kind of movement
different from gravitation,
19
Wealth, how created, 52; se-
cures leisure, 49; due to
genius, 147, 156
Wedding ring, 72
Whirl of dust, 35
Will, may be reduced to in-
significance, 121; is the first
individualising factor, 117
Wilno, 86
Wind power, 52
Wine, quality of, 30
Wisdom of blind men, 22
Wolves changed into dogs, 51
Words unspoken, 42, 43, 45
Working men as a class, 179
World of business, 124
Worship, of the gods of nature,
50; of material objects, 69
Wroński, 149
Wyspiański, 150

Xenophanes, 110

Younghusband, 144, 182, 183,
184, 186

Zeno of Elea, 10, 110
Zeus by Phidias, 32
Żółtowski, 148

203

For EU product safety concerns, contact us at Calle de José Abascal, 56–1°,
28003 Madrid, Spain or eugpsr@cambridge.org.